PHILOSOPHY OF SIKH RELIGION

a bunch of eleven studies

WAZIR SINGH

Ess Ess Publications

1981

Punjabi University, Patiala
First Published 1981

Rs.50.00

Published by: **S.K. Sethi** for Ess Ess **PUBLICATIONS**
4837/24, Ansari Road, New Delhi-110002.

Printed by: Ashokas Press, New Delhi-110005 at
Rashtravani Press, Maya Puri, New Delhi-110064.

To
Professor Ram Singh

FOREWORD

Ever since the decline of Sanskrit-based Udāsi and Nirmalā traditions of theological scholarship among Sikhs, rarely has an English-knowing Sikh sought admission to any of the Sikh theological seminaries run by conventional Sikh missions. Interestingly, even academic specialisation in Philosophy as a university subject has never been popular among Sikh alumni of the only University at Lahore before 1947, the Year of the Great Divide. Khazan Singh, Jodh Singh, Dr Mohan Singh, Teja Singh, Sahib Singh, G.S. Talib, Narain Singh, Gopal Singh, Daljeet Singh and quite a number of other scholars who have made a name in the field of Sikh Studies during the recent past, had no regular training in philosophy or theology proper. The few Sikh scholars who were able to graduate in the discipline of Philosophy and have since been able to contribute qualitatively to the small fund of Sikh literature, such as Sardars Kapur Singh and Sohan Singh, undertook the study of Sikh religion as a hobby. If, however, a scholar, such as the late Dr Sher Singh, chose to go in for higher research in the philosophy of Sikhism (he was awarded the degree of Ph.D. by the University of London on his thesis, later published under the title *Philosophy of Sikhism*), he had no choice to teach Sikh Philosophy and Religion in any institution, as none provided this facility at that time. Nor could he associate himself with any higher seat of learning as a whole-time research worker on any subject connected with Sikh Philosophy, as no University department was ready to offer whole-time work to any specialist in Sikh Studies.

It was after the partition of India and establishment of such seats of learning in the Indian Punjab as Punjabi University, Patiala and Guru Nanak Dev University, Amritsar that Sikh Studies, including religion and philosophy, were able to attract the attention of scholars interested in the study of Sikhism. Among the first set of scholars who have been able to avail of the new opportunity for work, Dr Wazir Singh's name is already well known to serious students of Sikh Studies. The bulk of his work, done before and after the acquisition of his doctorate on the subject of Humanism of Guru Nanak in 1970, is related to the understanding and interpretation of Sikh thought. Already he has to his credit publications, such as *Aspects of Guru Nanak's Philosophy* (1969), *Humanism of Guru Nanak* (1977), *Nanak-Bāni Chintan* (1969), *Guru Nanak Sidhānt* (1969), *Falsafā te Sikh Falsafā* (1980), to which will now be added his *Philosophy of Sikh Religion.*

The present work brings together eleven studies written either for seminars or for some learned journals, including Journal of Sikh Studies, Guru Nanak Dev University, Amritsar, Journal of Medieval Literature, Panjab University, Chandigarh, Indian Philosophical Quarterly, Poona, and Panchbati Sandesh, Dehra Dun. The comprehensive title of the present volume notwithstanding, this work will leave certain aspects of the philosophy of Sikh Religion untouched. Even so, Dr Singh concerns himself with such basic issues as the Sikh conception of Māyā, the Sikh Cosmology, Sikh Ethics, the elements of Sikh social thought and Sikh value-system. The questions raised by him are of global interest, especially for the students and teachers of comparative religion, who will find Dr Wazir Singh's grip over each subject quite strong and his presentation very lucid. That there are and will be other interpretations, is understandable, because the Sikh scripture contains, besides the complete works of their six Gurus, the selected compositions of a large number of Hindu and Muslim saints, some of whom lived even earlier than the founder-Guru in different parts of the Indian sub-continent and wrote in diverse linguistic idioms.

The reason why any attempt at codification of various aspects of Sikh Philosophy, has the seeds of controversy ingrained in it, is the emphasis of a writer on one text in preference to all other texts. For example, if a scholar chooses to establish determinism, he may select only such verses as help him prove his thesis, while some other scholar may prove that free-will is the Sikh thing alone. The selected texts will invariably be from the Scripture, but subjective preferences will make the balance tilt one way or the other. The authentic interpreter, on the other hand, has to be conversant not only with the idiom in which the texts were composed, but has to understand textual and contextual emphases, besides being an adept in decoding poetry into philosophy.

I am glad that Dr Wazir Singh is on the right path, trying to understand Sikh philosophy, as any modern mind would like to understand it. He knows the content of modern philosophy, and having been born in a family of interpreters and practisers of Sikh values, he has the benefit of knowing classical Sikhism at first hand. He writes not as a committed member of a faith talking to another committed colleague, but as an intellectual trying to introduce his findings about a sociological fact to equally non-committed fellow-intellectuals. The findings are meant to add to the existing knowledge of the readers; they will illumine certain dark recesses, but not having been written to convert people, those who revert to this work in search of passionate justification, may fail to find it there.

I am one of those admirers of Dr Wazir Singh's elucidations, who do not necessarily agree with all of them, but nonetheless regard them as valuable and welcome additions to the stock of Sikh literature which is now steadily increasing. Dr Singh has many creative years to go yet and it is natural to expect that this dedicated scholar, whose equal command over English and Punjabi languages and over the long-neglected Sikh conceptual area is enviable, will now undertake the challenging task of giving Sikh Philosophy its proper place in history on one hand and bringing out, if possible, its relevance to our own time, on the other.

Pritam Singh
Formerly Professor of Guru Nanak Studies
G.N.D. University, Amritsar

Patiala
October 24, 1980

CONTENTS

1

Philosophy of Sikh Religion

TASKS AND ISSUES

The central task of a philosophy of Sikh religion is to determine the nature of spiritual experience recommended by the mentors of Sikh faith. Their poetic compositions enshrined in the *Guru Granth*, the holy book compiled nearly four centuries earlier, enjoin upon the believers to lead the worldly life in a prescribed manner in order to obtain the valued experience. The inquiry must present the Sikh view of life, the inner core and identity of the religious beliefs of the Sikhs, and their evaluation. The text of the voluminous scripture, time and again, emphasizes a highly moral, almost a puritan, conduct of one's life, so much so that Sikh ethics would seem to occupy a status equivalent to the objective of spiritual realization. The question may be posed as to what is of fundamental importance in Sikhism, the experience or the way of life ? May be that the course of life in conformity with the teachings paves the way to a quintessence that is the goal; or may be the moral quality of life in itself constitutes the life of spirit for the Sikh.

Ethical and Spiritual Ideal

The problem, however, is not morality versus spirituality in Sikhism. It is the relative contribution and significance of each in the shaping of ideal human life. A scrutiny of the Sikh scriptures would reveal the twin-goal of *gurmukh* and *brahman-gyānī* for human beings to pursue. The former is an ideal man of faith, with complete orientation to the light of the Divine or the spiritual teacher designated as 'Guru'. The latter, namely *brahman-gyānī*, is a being possessed of absolute-consciousness, a completely enlightened soul, at par with the divine attribute of all-knowledge. In setting the ideal of a Divine-oriented fellow as well as of divinely conscious being, the Sikh scriptures seem to offer the alternative paths of devotion and vision, each leading in its own right to the heights of spiritual attainment. The *gurmukh* is essentially a man of moral excellence and virtue; of the world, yet non-attached; fearless, but full of compassion. An emotive quality characterizes his being. Through a highly affective state of the mind has he attuned himself to God of his faith. The *brahman-gyānī*, on the other hand, is essentially a man of enlightenment, of cosmic awareness, in full view of the mysterious dimensions of reality. If the *gurmukh* personifies, as it were, the ethical ideal, the *brahman-gyānī* is more nearly an embodiment of the philosophical ideal. A cognitive quality seems to characterize his person.

The Sikh Gurus, poet-philosophers as they were, in their depiction of *gurmukh* and *brahman-gyānī*, attributed to them qualities and descriptions that were interchangeable. The one shares largely in the attributes of the other, giving rise to the impression that *gurmukh* is not a category altogether distinct from *brahman-gyānī*. The path of loving devotion and the path of enlightenment seem to converge, resulting in the union of ethical and philosophical approaches in the religious life. The divine mystery is supposed to unfold itself as much to the man who loves as to the one who understands. Similarly, the man of absolute awareness is not devoid of affective or aesthetic sensibility; his vision is essentially the beatific vision. In the spiritual experience of the Sikh who makes the grade, ecstasy and altruistic motivation go together. The problem of choosing the more fundamental thesis out of *gurmukh's* love-oriented conduct and *brahman-gyānī's* spiritual insight, resolves itself in the state of equipoise that marks either of the two. The visionary's cosmic consciousness operates not simply on the conceptual plane; it is claimed to be a much-deeper illumination, intense enough to transform the ordinary faculties of cognition into the uniquely-gifted insight of sages and savants. An unusual perceptiveness is associated with men of mystical vision and devotion; they have the richness in their life of the direct experience of divine presence and its delight.

Religious Experience

In Sikhism, as in many other religious faiths, personal experience of the mystic's variety is admitted as authentic experience. According to the textual testimony, the content of this experience is not possible to express adequately through linguistic symbols. The impact that the experience leaves behind can, however, be articulated and described. We may form an impression, from such description, of the mental state of the individual undergoing the experience, but would fail to reproduce the actual state of mind in us, merely through a reading of the description. One may be in possession of words, but a direct vision of facts is another matter. The Gurus insist on one's having the authentic personal experience, and not the spurious thrill; they hold the spiritual experience to be qualitatively a distinct state, a direct communion with the infinite being, and a merger of one's individual existence with that being. The *brahman gyānī* knows what is meant to be experientially one with the ultimate,—merger of the drop in the ocean, or the ocean flowing through the drop.[1] In death, the finite is said to become part of the infinite; the individual spark is no more, the totality of fire is the reality that remains. But the religious experience of which the sages speak occurs during the lifetime of the individual so blessed, and not in death alone. The thrill is there, but it is an accompaniment. A sort of illumination inside takes place, the joy of which may faintly be compared with the aesthetic delight many people have under the impact of poetry or other art forms, as also on those rare occasions when a solution to some imaginative problem flashes through the mind like a quintessence.

1 *Guru Granth*, p. 878.

Some of the dimensions of religious experience recommended for the Sikh, apart from its transiency and ineffable character, include a sense of wonderfulness or ecstasy, the likeness of this experience to the experience of love between wife and husband, and the impact on society the religious experience leaves in the end. In the philosophy of Sikh religion, any lack of rational explanation for the riddle of life or origin of the universe, or for the sheer expanse and grandeur of nature, is not considered a fault or failure. Several hymns of the *Guru Granth* candidly affirm the futility of attempts at such calculations and explanations made in other sacred books. This may perhaps be viewed as indicative of an unscientific temper, but in the context of ultimate questions relating to the mysterious order of nature, it sounds saner not to venture authoritative answers. So far as the date of 'creation' of the world, or the number of stars and galaxies is concerned, the Sikh Gurus have expressly stated that the exact answer is known only to the Creator and to *none* else.[2] We at best can marvel and give expression to our sense of wonderfulness at the aspects of the macrocosmic as well as microcosmic realities disclosed to us.

It is also of interest to note that the relationship between the seeker of spiritual union with God as the divine Person postulated in Sikhism, is patterned on the marital relation between the woman and her loving and beloved husband, portrayed as the medieval lord of the wife's body and soul. The moods of a dedicated bride-in wait longing for the bissful embrace of her winsome man, stand for the emotions of a devoted *bhakta*, anticipating an undifferentiated unity with God. Hymns employing this kind of symbolism lend aesthetic colour to the depiction of religious feelings and speak of an enjoyment of God, as distinguished from a conceptual understanding of the experience involved. Why should the finite individual crave for uniting with an enduring or eternal spirit? And why should a human being take on the posture of a passive bride in the mystical experience? Perhaps one need not look for an answer or explanation on the discursive plane. Sikhism, in common with other faiths, simply alludes to the highest kind of blissfulness in one's

2 *Guru Granth*, p. 4.

intimate and lasting relationship with the permanent and most wonderful super being.[3]

Strictly speaking, the religious experience recommended by the the Sikh Gurus is not to be equated with the conventional practice or creed of mysticism. It is meant to be an experience that endures, that invests the individual with a vision of divine presence in the human community, and motivates him for dedicating himself to the welfare of fellow beings. The experience transforms him into an ideal man, viz. *gurmukh* or *brahman-gyānī*, whose charateristic mark is stated to be benevolence.[4] The Divine-oriented is in effect socially oriented. Repeated emphasis on contemplation and service, in the philosophy and culture of Sikhism, underlines the significance of an active public life, inspired and sustained by an illuminating vision. Spiritual experience though valuable in itself, the actual values to be promoted in life are determined through one's participation in the social milieu, under the direction of that experience.

The Status of God

Once it is admitted by a religious philosophy that God somehow enters into the personal experience of the individual,[5] questions in regard to the nature and existence of God become relevant for inquiry. Is it a supernatural being, beyond this world, that comes in the human experience, or is it an all-pervasive entity, immanent in the natural order? What kind of evidence is available to vouchsafe the existence of God? The position of Sikh thought on these and related issues has not been argued as much as asserted. The man of faith in Sikhism, as in other religions, simply accepts the beliefs put across in the scripture; it is for the theologian to offer rational justification for a particular set of beliefs. Systematic evaluation of religious beliefs and detailed scrutiny of their defence falls within the

3 *Vismād* and *Anand* stand for ecstasy and blissfulness in the *Gurbānī*.

4 For *par-upkār* (benevolence, altruism), see *Guru Granth*, pp. 273, 356 etc.

5 Cf. John Hick (Ed.) *Philosophy of Religion* (*Readings*), Prentice-Hall 1970, p. 533 (Appendix by the Editor).

province of philosophy of religion. The first task in this direction would be restatement of the position of Sikh religion, which claims to be not only a theistic but a monotheistic faith.

God of the Sikhs is both transcendent and immanent. The scripture is quite eloquent on this issue, whithout of course entering into argument. God's primordiality and state of absolute void are given poetic expression in some of the cosmologically rich hymns.[6] His powers of creation and His being the unmanifest origin and primal source of the manifest world, are asserted times without number. At the same time, the Divine is depicted, not only as coexisting with the world, but manifesting itself in and through the world. The highest of the high is stated to be present in the deepest caves of the human heart, and in all finite objects composing the universe, still in a process of continuous creation. If God were not immanent, and His nature was purely transcendent and external to the world, He could not be a knowable entity; even the world and human life would not be in existence to render a conception of Him possible. Even if both the natural and supernatural orders ran parallel, without the transcendent God ever descending to our day-to-day world, his existence would be meaningless to human life. The Gurus speak of God's positive presence in and around everyone of us.

Guru Nanak categorically asserts the supreme reality of his vision to be *Kartā purakh(u)*, i.e. Creator-person, who in His creativity is the necessary ground of the cosmic existence.[7] Yet, He is not merely an abstract power, infinite and timeless, or perfect and finished being-in-itself ; He is a Person, an embodiment of consiousness and freedom, love and grace. It is in this aspect that He is the object of worship and the protector and saviour of His creation. To the man of faith, the Divine stands in no need of proofs as to His existence; He just is there. The foremost evidence in favour of God's presence is the authority of the holy book. The latter suggests the specific course leading to an internal experience of God, and that would be the surest, first-hand testimony for the Sikh to rely upon. An

6 E.g. *Māru Solhe* hymns.

7 *Guru Granth*, pp. 1, 138, 448, 463.

intellectual probe into the ground of anyone's religious experience would fail to bear fruit, since none else can reconstruct, so it is claimed, the existential, concrete personal experience; at best, the inquiry would yeild clarification and interpretation of the concepts and symbols involved.

The *Guru-Granth*, not strictly a philosophical treatise, does not adduce any of the theistic arguments to prove the existence of God. However, it contains sufficient material that might be quoted in support of ontological, cosmological, teleological or other conventional 'proofs'. The hymns repeatedly refer to the greatest and highest being that the human mind can possibly conceive. He is the origin and first cause of all that exists; His ordinance pervades the entire universe. He is the sole author of nature, with all its colour, variety and design. Since God is credited with the assigning of both order and purpose to nature, the position of *Guru-bānī* may be interpreted as affirming a cosmoteleological argument.[8] Man, wondering at the miracle of creation, can only sing the praises of its benevolent architect; his duty is to cognize the divine ordinance and live up to it.

x x x

Philosophy of religion, in general, is of the view that whatever evidence could be produced in favour of God's existence, would have to be indirect (like our present evidence for electrons),[9] since God cannot be seen face to face. Philosophy of Sikh religion, relying on the 'living spring' of religious experience,[10] draws its vitality from this very source, notwithstanding the skeptical objection that an individual's private, inner experience can provide no guarantee for the existence of a divine being. For the critic, religious experience is not a distinctive cognitive activity of man;[11] as a form of existential commitment, religious

8 Cf. *The Journal of Religion*, Chicago, 10-1976: "A Rationale for a Cosmoteleological Argument for God," by Peter A. Bertocci.

9 Cf. John Hospers in *An Introduction to Philosophical Analysis*, Prentice-Hall (Allied, New Delhi, 1971), p. 490.

10 Phrase used by John Hick, op. cit., p. 537.

11 Cf. Randall, "A Form of Religious Naturalism," in John Hick (Ed.), op. cit.

devotion may bear the fruits of social virtues; all human concern with God, and conceptions of his power and perfection etc., are nothing but verbal symbols. The humanist perspective views the problem of religion, not as the problem of God, but of man; religion is the embodiment of mankind's higher aspirations. The Sikh doctrine of religion, however, would seem to agree with the view of religion as 'man's ultimate concern for the Ultimate,' and with the view of God as the ground of our being.[12]

Some of the issues of special interest for a philosophy of Sikh religion, apart from the nature of spiritual experience, God, and religious faith, concern the role and efficacy of prayer, concepts of divine grace, status of good and evil in the worldly life, and questions of human destiny, death and immortality. Some of the peripheral issues like miracles and paradise, and socio-cultural issues of religious observances, also call for scrutiny and evaluation. Besides, a philosophical study of Sikhim would address itself to the problem of religious language; it would examine the symbolic expressions used in the scriptural text, e.g. *karam-khand, sach-khand, oamkār, hukam* and relate them to the individual's experience, so as to determine their meaning and value for the adherent. Evaluation of the attempts made from time to time to put new constructions on the tenets and beliefs of Sikhism, in order to harmonize them with the spirit of modern science, is one of the other tasks to be taken up by a philosophy of Sikh religion.

12 Both phrases are from Paul Tillich, *Systematic Theology*, Chicago, 1951.

Philosophy of the Mool-Mantra

The *mool mantra* is a philosophic testimony of Guru Nanak's poetic vision of the supreme reality. The *mantra* consists of fourteen sybmols through which the Guru projects the nature, potentialilties and values of the Being of his vision. The equivalent symbols that may be used in the interpretation of his terms are indicated below :

Ek	The Absolute Spirit
Oamkār	The Protector/Lord Supreme
Sat(i)	Reality Eternal
Nām(u)	Manifest in Truth
Kartā	Principle of Creation
Purakh(u)	Divine Person
Nirbhau	Controlled by none
Nirvair(u)	Contradicted by none
Akāl	Reality Transcending Time
Moorat(i)	Immanent in Cosmic Form
Ajooni	Not cast in the womb
Saibham	Self-Installed
Gur	Enlightener of All
Prasād(i)	Grace for all

2. I have called the symbols of the *mool mantra* a 'philosophic' testimony. The reason is twofold. Guru Nanak has

symbolized, through them, his philosophic quest for the articulation of spiritual experience. It is not in the fashion of a scientist's quest for the truth; he is not aiming at the acquisition of knowledge that may be logically formulated, or from which demonstrable conclusions are to be drawn. Whatever he has expressed cannot be judged as 'true' or 'false' in the narrow technical sense of the propostitions of science. Yet, all what he has said, through the 14 constituents of his *mool mantra*, is knowledge in philosophic sense. It is a concise statement of the conceptual framework of a new religious faith. The second part of the reason is that the symbols employed by Guru Nanak, readily lend themselves to metaphysical interpretation. Nearly all of them have a tradition of philosophic-theistic beliefs held in India and, in the form of their counterparts, in the West as well.

3. Why have I characterized the vision of Guru Nanak as 'poetic'? Because it is an insight into the nature of Being that has revealed to us a number of its attributes, but which is not an intellectual inquiry making use of scientific methods and directed towards a balanced, reasoned out, logical structure. Ostensibly, the *mool mantra* seems to have attempted a description of the objectively real, in a detatched manner, without any subjective commitment. But if such were the case some evidence of empirical observation might have been adduced, some argumentation should have been employed and a rational construction placed on the object of examination. Its further implication would be that Guru Nanak proceeded without an inner, personal experience. But the quality of his poetry leaves little doubt as to the depth of his vision and intimate grasp of the reality depicted in his verse. The symbolism employed to express the features of this reality is indicative of the existential experience gone through, and not merely an abstract, impersonal portrayal of the object of rational choice. His was essentially a religious experience, and hence experience of an existential situation.

4. The first part of the *mool mantra*, comprising the group of four elements of *ek*, *oamkār*, *sat*(*i*) and *nām*(*u*), presents an

integrated view of the ultimate reality that is subject to metaphysical and religious interpretation simultaneously. In fact, the symbols *ek* (the One) and *sat*(*i*) (the Real) refer to the Absolute of philosophy, and the symbols *oamkār* (the Providence) and *nām*(*u*) (the True) refer to the Absolute of religion. All the four are indicative of the ontological status that Guru Nanak chose to give to the Supreme Being. The numeral 1 (one) represents the single, Undifferentiated Essence or Spirit which is the unmanifest, formless Absolute. The symbol *oamkār*, on the other hand, represents the expressed power of Being, in its differentiated, manifest forms. The combination of *ek-oamkār*, on the whole, is therefore indicative of the one-many, unmanifest-manifest, Absolute-cum-God. This may remind one of the Advaitic *Brahman Ishvar* pair, but in Shankar the personified Ishvar is ultimately assimilated into the impersonal Absolute or Brahman. Not so in Guru Nanak. He makes no attempt to reduce one into the other. Both retain their position and importance as aspects of the same single system.

5. The symbol *Oamkār*, as derived from the tri-syllabic symbol *Oam* (a-u-m), represents the holiest of all sounds, in the Indian tradition. It stands for the primordial sound (sabda), implying Sabda-Brahman, i.e. the Divine himself. *Oamkār* is also interpreted as the Protector, which implies 'Lord Supreme' of the phenomenal world. In this sense, *Oamkār* is intrinsically related to the concept of existence in all its dimensions. The universe is sustained and supported by a conscious Being who is the Providence. He is one with existence; the word is but a personification of Him; or to put it differently He is immanent in the universe of infinite forms. This universe cannot be chaotic; being the expression of one single power or essence, it must be capable of unification in a single system. It is, therefore, an ordered universe or cosmos. Its contents are arranged in a polyphasic unity, from lower to higher orders, ultimately reaching the oneness of the Absolute. That explains the comprehensibility of the world-order, its rational character, its intelligibility to the human mind, which itself is a product and part of the nature's system. It is the manifest aspect or Truth that is revealed to the human agency

of science, in the form of the processes of nature. In discovering the universe and its laws, science is becoming aware of the Providence; in realizing the truth of existence, man is reaching out to his ultimate concern and support.

6. The fact that *Oamkār* in the *mool mantra* is preceded by 1 (one) shows that in spite of the many-ness of the revealed world, its oneness is not to be lost sight of. It is monistic in character, though pluralistic in content. It is many, yet one. But it is one, and not zero. Guru Nanak's choice of the numeral 1 (one) is an unmistakable indication of his characterization of the highest reality as positive essence, in contrast with the negativism of *sunyavād* or nihilism. It is presence and affirmation, not negation. The world emanates from the positive essence; as such it is a real world, and not merely an illusion. A world in which the Providence is immanent, cannot be pure falsehood. Thus, the living, all-extensive, all-comprehensive reality, which is unitary, yet multifaeed, is the object of estimation in the *mool mantra*. Those scholars who interpret *Ek-Oamkār* as the Sikh Trinity, and believe it to be a combination of Ek-Oam-Akār, do not fail to take into consideration the 'form' (*akār*) of the created world whose reality is affirmed. In the very next symbol of *sat*(*i*), Guru Nanak has actually described it as the Real. In philosophical terms, it is the basic substance of all the modes of existence; it is the reality of the things and forms of the world. Here Guru Nanak seems to be emerging from the plane of intuitive faith to that of philosophic belief. He had the vision of a power expressing itself as the Being, immanent in the world-order. Now, he is considering this power as the really real, the focus of all, that is, the ultimate object of all pursuit of knowledge.

7. Guru Nanak has combined the symbol *sat*(*i*) with the symbol *nām*(*u*) which literally means 'name'. Here again, the implication of the existent world-order is clear. When we refer to the world of names and forms, we refer to the concrete, empirical universe which we know in our ordinary experience and discover through the agency of science. In short, *nām* (*u*) is truth, or the knowable aspect of Reality. It represents the

natural order, corresponding to the symbol *Oamkār*. *Nām*(*u*) accordingly is of the nature of *Ishvar* or God, immanent in the universe. Whatever is, is *nām*(*u*). But the world as a totality may be conceived in terms of a process, a moving and developing universe which is not a finally perfect order of things. What, then, is the status of God conceived as Truth? The universe is neither complete nor perfect. Can we say that God's nature too lacks completeness and perfection, since God's is identical with the universe? If the universe is developing, the nature of God must also be developing; if the world is finite, so must be the Divine? However, taken in the literal sense, *Ṅām* (name) stands for the designation of *sat*(*i*) i.e. the eternal reality. But it is evidently not a functional name indicating any of the attributes or operations of that reality. It may be taken in the sense of the 'primordial name'—which is Reality Eternal (or *satya*), and refers to the preceding symbols of *Ek* and *Oamkār*.

8. Most of us, I imagine, who are accustomed to thinking of God in absolute terms, as the perfect, unsurpassable Being, might experience a sense of shock at the description of God in terms of relatively perfet, or a finite being. Recent philosophy, however, has experimented with the concept of a finite God, or God in the making. If the universe is not a closed or finished entity then the universe of tomorrow would not be the same as of today. God who is identical with the universe of today, will not, therefore, be identical with the universe of tomorrow, unless He also develops and identifies Himself with the changed universe. Hence, the concept of the developing nature of God, that is, an unfinished Being in process, or God that is becoming, unfolding, actualizing His potentialities. We may assert, for the sake of argument, that a good person is one who suffers at the spectacle of evil or suffering of others. If God is good then He must suffer with the suffering of worldly beings. But in that event, He will not be absolute bliss, since His bliss would be tempered by suffering, wpich is negation of bliss. In case He remains in bliss, in spite of the suffering of mankind, what kind of a good God is He!—so runs the argument.

9. Those of the idealist philosophers who conceive the

Absolute as the necessary, supreme and infinite Being. regard the universe as phenomenal, conditioned and finite. The world is contingent as against reality that is necessary, but the world is ultimately absorbed into the Absolute, since the two cannot be divorced from each other. Evidently, then, the necessary and infinite Being contains the contigent and finite within itself. The aspect that is superemely real or *sat(i)*, is indissoluby associated with the aspect that is phenomenal or *nām(u)*. Thus the *sat(i) nām(u)* of the *mool mantra* may be interpreted as the Real-cum-Apparent, Infinite-Finite, Being-Becoming. It does not mean that the Divine Being lacks perfection; it only implies that in His phenomenal aspect He is finite, whereas in His transcendental aspect He is infinite and perfect. When Whitehead presents the bipolar nature of God, he is combining the flux and process of the world with the permanence and reality of the Divine. To him, God is the selective principle, according to which eternal objects are picked out from the realm of possibility and placed in the realm of actuality. The primordial nature of God is the conceptual pole. He is the Ground of all rationality, and is the eternal, transcendental Absolute. The consequent nature of God is the physical pole; He is the immanent God, the source and saviour of the actual physical world, a factor within reality.

10. In the second part of the *mool mantra*, Guru Nanak counted eight attributes of the Divine Being. He starts with the creative principle (*kartā*) which to the Indian tradition is known as Brahmā. This attribute of God, supported by a majority of theologians in the East and the West, is nonetheless attacked by the contemporary movement of 'process, theology' and mataphysics of critical naturalism. God does not stand outside the flow of time; nor is He the creator of the universe *ex nihilo*. Naturalism is prepared to admit God as coexistent with the totality of nature or universe; but a perfect, eternal and transcendent God, it asserts, is an unwarranted interpretation of the religious experience of certain individuals. Guru Nanak, however, attributes positive creativity to his God. Combined with the symbol *Purakh*, the symbol *Kartā* means the Creator-Divine Person. The world of nature is not taken to be beginningless

(*anādi*), or self created; it is the creation (*rachnā*) of the Creator Person.

11. Another significant feature of the highest reality, according to Guru Nanak, is consciousness, which is clear from its characterization as Person (*purakh*(*u*)). It may be asked, to which aspect of reality personality is attributed—to the Absolute of philosophy, or to the God of religion? The Indian tradition favours the concept of *sat-chit-ānand*, that is, it treats the Absolute as reality, consciousness and bliss. The implication is that the Supreme Being does not *possess* consciousness, but rather it *is* consciousness. It is not merely 'It' but 'He', which means a person. As consciousness, He may be the Ground of rationality and order in the universe. He is the cosmic consciousness, in the sense of prosonification of the cosmos that is self-aware. But is it not just a projection of the human mind that is termed 'cosmic awareness'? Is it not, as Feuerbach believed, that man has created God in his own image, as a person endowed with consciousness? Thought, according to Spinoza, is one of the infinite number of attributes of the divine substance, which is nothing but nature. Is it nature that is depicted as *purakh* in the *mool mantra*? We cannot, here, fail to remember that Guru Nanak's Supreme Being is Creator or *kartā* as well. He, as the creator of the natural order, also identifies Himself with His creation. He is *kartā*-cum-*purakh*, that is, He is the conscious creative force; not merely an abstract principle, but a living and thinking Being possessed of personal qualities.

12. The next pair of attributes, *nirbhau* and *nirvair(u)* are ordinarily interpreted in a way that brings the Divine Person down to exclusively human level. To say that God is not affraid of anyone, and bears no enmity to anyone, does not do justice to the concept of the realmost entity. *Bhau* is not merely 'fear', it is control and discipline as well. Similarly, *vair* is not simply enmity: it also means opposition and contradiction. Guru Nanak seems to imply that the Absolute is unsurpassable and hence under the discipline of none. A higher and more authoritative being is unthinkable. As God, He is not in subor-

dination to anyone; He is absolutely free. In *sat-chit-ānand*, the highest reality is characterized as 'bliss', which is also rendered as 'freedom'. God does, as He pleases; He is not bound by any limitations; all rules and principles emanate from Him, since He is the Ground of all thought and reason. This uncontrolled, un-disciplined Being is also the un-contradicted Being. No logical contradictory of Him is possible; it makes no sense to say that there is a non-Being as opposed to Being. Guru Nanak conceives the Absolute as unique and affirmative. There is no match for Him; there is no negation of Him.

13. The symbols of *akāl* and *moorat* (*i*) seek to convey the featureless reality that has features as well. Literally, *akāl* is non-temporal, that is, not governed by time, above and beyond the process of time and history, or simply eternal. The empirical world of names and forms is temporal; all modes of existence are events occurring along the long vista of universal history. To put it differently, time is the creative force; all this wondrous show of the world is a product of time. In the polarity between time and eternity, time is conceived as motion, as process, whereas eternity is motionless, ever the same. Laws of motion bring into being the forms and modes of physical existence. But no such laws apply to the ultimate reality, which therefore remains formless and featureless. Then, what is it ? Simply void ? Simply negation or zero ? Guru Nanak at once adds, the featureless, non-temporal reality appears in form also; it acquires all the features of image or *moorat*(*i*). It is eternal, yet in form. It is both time and eternity, developing and beyond development; or in Whitehead's terminology, Process and Reality.

14. Then follow the attributes of *ajooni* and *saibham*, i.e. non-born and self-installed. The Divine Person is not subject to biological evolution; He need not develop the features of higher organisms in the manner of animal species. If He is above the temporal process that governs the physical universe, He also transcends the process that gives birth to animate beings. Then, how does He appear in tangible form; if He has no designer, no maker, no parent, who brings Him into existence, who installs and establishes Him ? The answer

is—Himself. The unmanifest has the capacity for manifestation, for self-expression and self-installation. This automatic establishment in the concrete form is the unique feature of the otherwise subtle and featureless reality. No other entity, creature or being shares this potentiality of Guru Nanak's Absolute.

15. After presenting the nature and attributes of the Divine substance of his poetic vision, Guru Nanak enters the realm of values. If the Absolute is possessed of unique, unshared powers, what does it matter to us ? If He has nothing to do with mankind, how is He relevant to human life ? But Guru Nanak brings man into relationship with his benevolent Providence. As the ultimate source of system and order in the universe, God enlightens the human mind and equips it for the discovering of the cosmic order. In this respect, He is the divine Teacher (Guru), who guides the destiny of man, shows him the path of life, and gives him freedom of choice and action in the framework of temporal existence. Not only that He is the enlightener, the Divine Person of Guru Nanak's vision is also gracious. He is embodiment of Grace itself. It is His grace, *prasād*(*i*) that the order of nature is unfolding itself, that evolution has led to the emergence of mankind with powers of intelligent activity and self-consciousness. It is through divine grace that man is in a position to seek and promote values, that he is enabled to experience the divine in nature as well as in the deepest caves of his own self. Some theologians prefer to combine 'Gur' and 'Prasād' in order to infer the meaning that the absolute reality can be realized through the grace of the 'guru'—i.e. the spiritual mentor. Yet another interpretation of the symbol 'prasād' is the customary phrase "by the grace of" —serving as a poetic invocation of the Supreme Reality symbolically depicted in the *mool-mantra*. Such an interpretation sounds reasonable when the *mantra* stands at the head of a text composed "by the grace of" one absolute spirit, enlightener etc.

16. The *mool-mantra*, as an expression of Guru Nanak's intuitive insight into the metaphysical realm, presents an integrated view of the basic reality that is monistic, but whose manifestation is pluralistic. The conceptual framework of the

mantra is comprehensive enough to include ten of the most significant attributes of the Absolute, with the last two belonging to the realm of values with its humanistic import. The extent and magnitude of the non-temporal creative principle can scarcely be estimated by a phenomenal being subject to the space-time order. Even the manifest aspect of this unmanifest Spirit, namely the physical universe or process of nature, defies measure and count. Perhaps, the Divine Person alone can contemplate the vastness and totality of the cosmic existence. Man, however, is fortunately placed in sharing a capacity for the experience of this endless mystery. He may be well advised to expand his mental universe so as to reflect, in an increasing measure, the vastness and magnitude of the reality of his philosophic contemplations. That would be the true meaning of 'cosmic consciousness', from the human point of view. It would be man's awareness of the entirety of the Cosmic Being. Guru Nanak assures us that the light and grace of the Divine Enlightener are ever with man in his search.

3

Guru Nanak's Conception of Maya

Māyā belongs to the class of concepts that have acquired the status of philosophic categories. In the philosophy of naturalism, for instance, nature is regarded as the ultimate category, and reality to the super nature or transcendent being is denied. By contrast, the idealist asserts consciousness, experience or idea as the sole category of his metaphysics. These fundamental modes of existence, or ultimate principles of understanding and experience, are, in the final analysis, products of the human mental activity. They do not refer so much to one or another of the entities in the external world, as to the speculative realm of man's life. All philosophy, in this sense, is play of concepts supported by fancy and argument, and inspired by purposes that embrace the truths of life, the universe, or the totality of being. In one of the attempts to comprehend the nature of reality, some of the philosophic minds in India invented the concept of māyā and, with the help of this child of speculation, offered an alternative interpretation of the world inhabited by man, adding to the charming diversity of theories contending for supremacy.

One of the thinkers and exponents of the characteristically Indian view of life, who not only continued the māyā tradition of thought in his own way, but contributed to its enrichment, was the poet-philosopher Guru Nanak. He employed the concept of māyā in his poetry as part of his repertory, in order to bring home to mankind his message of ethico-spiritual life. As distinct from his predecessors in the region of philosophy proper, and in line with the poet-devotees, Guru Nanak extended the area of application of the term *māyā* by adopting it as a symbol in the conceptual framework of his poetry. He was not bound, in his poetic freedom, by the strictly metaphysical nuances of the term. Rather, he moulded the concept of māyā to the needs of his composition and its content, making use of it in a symbolic sense to communicate his image of evil, sometimes investing the term with an enhanced meaning through its combination with another component, as in *moh*-māyā, māyā-*mamtā*, etc.

Subject-Object of Maya

The problem of māyā in philosophy is intimately linked with some of the other metaphysical problems, such as subject-object, appearance and reality, man and God. It is also connected with the issue of knowledge and ignorance. Māyā is variously described as a veil or curtain concealing reality; appearance of the phenomenal world as against things-in-themselves; the grand illusion or the cosmic principle of illusion. In any case, it makes a necessary reference to living beings, in particular to man, whose vision is obscured by the spell of māyā, or to whom the manifold world comes as an illusory experience. Māyā as ignorance is essentially human ignorance or, more pointedly, that of an individual who has yet to work his way to illumination and knowledge. In brief, māyā is assumed to stand between man and reality, producing error and illusion in the human mind, and creating difficulties in the individual's way to a state of knowledge and bliss. Thus conceived, it is the Indian counterpart of the devil, the evil incarnate.

Guru Nanak-*bāni* presents māyā from the objectivist as well as the subjectivist points of view. Firstly, as in common parlance, the term *māyā* denotes wealth or riches. An individual engrossed in the worldly possessions is *māyādhāri* who remains oblivious of the spiritual aspect of life. Such a one is castigated as blind and deaf in the *bāni*. Secondly, attractions of the worldly life, in general, are characterized as māyā. Their spell is cast not only on human beings, but on all forms of life, including *devi* and *deva* who long for the enjoyment of worldly charms. Thirdly, the phenomenal world or the universe itself is māyā which is identical with nature at all levels—physical, biological, mental—created and established by the Divine ordinance. This view depicts māyā at the height of objectivity, as a living, operating, seemingly endless, and colourful world of names and forms. Human consciousness, which is a part of the phenomenal world of māyā, not only mirrors this world, but engages itself in the un-covering of its depths and the dis-covering of its truths. All human endeavour, common sense and reason, all science and philosophy, all technological ventures and probes form part of the struggle to solve the riddle of this empirical but mysterious world.

If the external world of sense and inference symbolizes māyā as the object, the inner, mental world of man represents māyā as the subject. In the Nanak-*bāni*, one prominent subjective aspect of māyā is the passionate self of man—his sensuous, possessive, egoistic nature. Another aspect is represented by human attachment with the world—the *moh*-māyā or infatuations which prevent man from rising above his individuality and relativity. However, the summit of māyā's subjectivity is shown as ignorance—the true character of māyā, which also provides foundation to the doctrine of Illusionism. Here, the objective and the subjective of māyā converge : the phenomenal world appears to human consciousness, and consciousness is of the phenomena of nature. Neither the external world nor human exprience is real : both are illusory. Māyā is reflecting māyā. Human ignorance indulges in the fanciful building up of the world of appearance. The subject (ignorance) is hooked up with the object (illusion)—both products of māyā and both identical with māyā.

The Traditional View

In considering the approach of Guru Nanak to the question of māyā, it may be asked which of the two aspects, the subjective and the objective, has been emphasized in his *bāni*. One interpretation classifies Guru Nanak with the exponents of the

Advaita Vedānta school. This line of thinking strives to demon strate the falsity of the world, considering it as the product of a creative illusion that is māyā. Reality on this view is non-dual; it is Brahman or the Absolute; nothing other than Brahman really exists or is really real. The other major interpretation of Guru Nanak's faith seeks to affirm that the natural world is real and true; it is the product of God's creativity and cannot be dismissed as a mere illusion. God himself has assumed the manifest form of the cosmic order. The failure on our part to view the universe as God in his immanent aspect, is due to our ignorance or infatuation, which is nothing but māyā.

It is true that the Advaitic doctrine considers māyā from the subjective point of view and explains it in terms of *avidyā* or ignorance of the human soul. When the individual frees himself from the influence of māyā, he awakes to the reality of a single non-dual, eternal Brahman. To him, māyā is no more; it has come to an end. However, this is one part of the story. The other part treats of māyā as *aṇādi* or beginningless; it is also indescribable. The world of names and forms is a product of māyā, which is indicative of māyā's unique powers of creation and of concealing reality. It is māyā that misleads the human soul into taking a distorted view of the essential reality. The human soul is of the same character as the universal Spirit, that is Brahman, but the influence of māyā does not allow the individual to pierce the veil and realize this identity. He goes on mistaking the world as real in itself. This part of the theory portrays māyā as an objective entity whose nature, though partially grasped, remains on the whole indeterminate.

Thus, the Advaitic category of māyā is designed to serve as the fundamental mode of existence endowed with supreme powers. Its being is conceived as parallel to that of Brahman, for both are treated as beginnigless and beyond adequate expression. Only to a spiritually advanced individual māyā ceases to be, and Brahman alone remains. By implication, māyā continues to exist for the rest of mankind. Its objectivity and its powers of creation and deception must last as long as any of the spiritually less evolved creatures inhabit any part of the universe. It is this extreme objectification of māyā in the Vedantic theory, to which Guru Nanak does not seem to subscribe. He does not assign to it the character of a metaphysical category in the framework of his poetic compositions.

Maya and Natural Order

In his references to the external world, Guru Nanak has employed the terms *jagat* (or *jag*), *duniyā*, *srishti* (or *sirthee*), *khand-brahmand*, *qudrat*, as also *māyā*. Some other terms e.g. *lok*, *sūnya*, *khel* and *rachanā* also find place in the *bāni*. All of these may be interpreted as referring to the creativity of the Divine. The phenomenal world emanates from Him and is the manifestation of His formless essence. The Guru refers to the entire world of observation as *māyā-chhāyā*—implying that the universe is not an ever-lasting entity; it is shadowy in character, subject to the temporal process, and destined to end in 'four days'—as figuratively put. This emphasis on the ephemerality and non-permanence of the cosmic order is perhaps the key to the interpretation of Guru Nanak's conception of māyā and the world. Māyā is that of which the essence is time; it has come into being at the will of the Divine, and must disappear when He so ordains. In other words, nature as creation is neither beginningless nor self-sufficient. It rests in the Creator, whose embodiment it is.

Thus, māyā and nature (*qudrat*) seem identical in the Nanak-*bāni*. The world of nature may be taken as māyā incarnate, denying any special or extraordinary existence to māyā. This amounts to asserting that the world exists in its own right as established by the Divine Will, and not as a product of some supposed intermediary, namely māyā. It also means that the order of nature is not to be considered an illusion, pure and simple. We must not associate any real value with the phenomenal world, because, as the teaching goes, it is not ever-lasting or eternal. However, it may be 'illusory' in the sense that it appears to us permanent, whereas its real status is that of creation. Accordingly, the world is not rejected as illusion in the Nanak-*bāni*, in spite of its occassional characterization in terms of māyā or *chhāyā*, or an edifice of smoke, etc. It is the *qudrat* of the *Qādir* whose creativity is not in doubt anywhere in the *bāni*.

In the Western philosophy, Plato is credited with the view that treats of the phenomenal world as a veil or illusion. But Plato shows keen interest in the world and its affairs, especially the socio-political and moral life of the people. His rejection of the space-time world is only partial and is based on his dislike for sensory knowledge. In his attempt to establish the superiority of the rational faculty in cognizing the higher truths, he posited an ideal world of immutable essences, which formed the foundation for the imitative world of phenomena that was 'unreal'. The objective idealism of the modern period does not assume another world that is real, apart from the world known to us in our commonsense experience. Its point of departure is the view that reality belongs to the concrete whole and not to any part abstracted from it. Parts are appearances treated as physical, biological, etc. The whole or the Absolute is 'experience' itself, which affirms the spiritual or ideal nature of reality. The Absloute is taken as the single self-differentiating system, characterized by harmony and comprehensiveness.

In the first view, the order of nature is an imitation of the heavenly world of essences, whereas the second view considers nature as an appearance of the all-inclusive reality. By contrast, Guru Nanak's view presents nature as an order of creation, with the immanent creative Spirit observing it in freedom and joy. The self-differentiating principle of the Absolute, in the idealist theory, assumes in the *bāni* the figure of self installation of the supreme Self in the form of the natural order of diversity and multiple entities. Guru Nanak's cosmology views the cosmos as a manifestation of the unmanifest, a truthful embodiment of the supremely real, a concrete image of the power of Being that was pure spirituality, variously depicted as the Void, the Formless, the primordial Origin and the true. The creative principle is symbolized as *Oaṁkaar*, *Nām*, as also the *Qādir*. The illusionism of the māyā-theory is thus replaced with the principle of creativity and of self-manifestation.

The Governing Principle of Nature

The universe of Guru Nanak's conception may be interpreted as emanating from the individuating principle of ego in man, as alluded to in the *Sidha-Gosht*. If so, the world must be governed by processes of the human mind. However, this interpretation scarcely accords with the general intent of the *bāni* except in the sense that the appearance of the world cannot be dissociated from experience. Some sort of mental energy must be present to *experience* the existence; in the absence of sentient capacity, no allusion to or assertion of any sort of reality is possible. However, acceptance of a relation between existence and experience does not entail dependence of the former on the latter. How does the world *appear*? It appears in the consciousness of living beings. But, who is the author of the world? Not human ego; it is the Supreme itself. Accordingly, the governing principle of nature is the Ordinance of the Divine, the *hukam*, that maintains the elements, the land and waters, the stars and planets, in fact the entire spatio-temporal cosmos and its processes. All matter, life and mind obey the discipline of that single absolute authority which transcends all discipline, control or order. All else is under the 'fear' of the One that is fearless in Himself.

Guru Nanak depicts the powers of the Divine in numerous dimensions, according to the poetic mood of the occasion. Sometimes he is addressing the Creator in his personified aspect, as the author of the universe that is true. Whatever He has established, cannot be false or unreal. Rather, the True one himself has taken on the garb of the manifest nature. On other occasions, the creative power is portrayed as the Void, the formless indeterminate Being, whose nature is beyond estimation or intelligibility. The extent of His Ordinance can hardly be imagined and measured, howsoever the wise, in their wisdom, and poets in their fancy may try. Guru Nanak, himself a poet of the highest order, expresses a deep sense of mystery and ecstasy when he comes to viewing the vastness of creation and its origin. Yet, there are occasions when he presents the outlines of his vision of the cosmic evolution, in terms of the air, water and fire originating from their only source that is Truth, bringing into being the multi-dimensional world of ours. Or it may be in terms of the nebulous darkness that prevailed while the formless Void remained in trance, prior to his act of creation; naught was in existence then, neither land nor skies, neither gods nor men, neither faith nor knowing; when the unmanifest so willed, the process of nature came into play and became manifest with countless facets and apperances. The creative and governing principle of the universe is nothing but the inscrutable will of the mystery that is Divine.

Of course, the figures of Brahmā, Vishnu and Shiva, as also of māyā frequently find place in the *bāni*, indicative of the link with the tradition of Indian thought. But these figures stand for the powers of the Divine in the framework of Guru Nanak's diction. Brahmā cannot be taken in the literal sense of a creator with absolute authority. Likewise, māyā as an independent creative power would be out of place with the spirit of Nanak-*bāni*. The only agency that governs the process of nature is nature itself as an embodiment of the Divine Ordinance. If this aspect of nature were to be identified as māyā, in the objective sense, no contradiction would be involved, since the existence of nature is recognized in the *bāni* in the form of '*qudrat*' of the *Qādir*. However, if nature is viewed as an independent realm, final in itself, then the interpretation fails to cohere with Guru Nanak's over-all view of reality. He himself describes such a world as false—that is, a world which is falsely viewed as real in itself, without the presence of its creative Spirit. The thrust of the poetic depiction seems to be that the world is real if the Divine immanence is realized in every part and corner of it; the same world is false and unreal if we fail to observe Him residing in the natural order.

Ultimately, therefore, it is left to the human individual to look at the universe as mere nature devoid of God, or to view it as imbued with his spiritual presence. Guru Nanak teaches man to adopt a way of life consistent with the intuitive vision of theistic immanence. Such a vision results in the ordering of the multiplicity of forms into a systematic unity. Alternatively, the world of plurality without a unifying principle of harmony and coherence, is indicative of a vision confined to sense experience alone; it is governed by the individuating influence of the human ego. The Nanak-*bāni* is a costant reminder of the limits imposed upon man by his native ignorance; it serves to awaken him to the spiritual turth of existence and its governing principle, namely the Divine Will. The order of nature that appears to the subjectivity of the individual is māyā. Its essence, according to the *bāni,* is not within the reach of the ego. It is only when the inner vision is in tune with the essence-in-existence that māyā is dispelled, and illumination of the self is attained.

is nothing more than a manifestation or externalization of the absolute Spirit. Its physical appearance is correlated to human understanding with all its limitations of here-and-now. In essence, the world is of the nature of *experience*, that is, in the supra-empirical sense of the term. Here, the natural is reduced to the supernatural The metaphysical import of *Gurbānī*, with its concepts of Divine Will, Creativity and Omnipresence, fits in well with the idealist position. As opposed to this, the reductionist operation performed by the materialist, who seeks to explain the mental and the spiritual in terms of matter-in-motion, goes contrary to the perspective of *Gurbānī*. The Gurus seem to view nature as a creative force with its own regulations and procedures, but ultimately acting as the organ or agency of the divine Creator, whose writ is final. The world of nature is not illusory on this view, since the self-expression of the realmost Being, cannot but be real itself.[3] Even if the world were a sport or mere play, it is the *real* play of the Divine.[4] "This world is the abode of Truth; the True one resides herein."[5]

Facts and Values

Comprehension of fact and pursuit of value are among the important functions of the human psyche. The Gurus, however, did not emphasize the mere grasp or cognition of fact, since it was not their business, as spiritual leaders of men, to do so. But the pursuit of value naturally became the object of their most vigorous emphasis. The supreme mission of their life seemed to promote intuitive awareness of a value that transcended other values of human life, both high and low, narrow and wide. This comprehensive, all transcending value that the human soul could rely upon for ultimate support, was doubtlessly the Divine itself. Emotionally pursued, it became the object of the highest devotion and realization; rationally conceived, it served as the farthest limit of comprehension, namely

3 *Ap sat(i) kīā sabh(u) sat(i)* (*Guru Granth*, p. 294)
4 ...*Sachā khel tumārā* (*Guru Granth*, p. 764)
5 *Ih(u) jag(u) sachai ki haī kothari sache kā vich(i) vās(u)* (*Guru Granth*, p. 463)

Brahman or the Absolute. It could also be designated as the supreme, eternal, spiritual Reality, or *Sat-Chit-Ānand* of the Indian conception.

Thus visualized, the Divine acquires the status of the highest value that man can experience in the inmost depths of his person. It may be viewed as a Being greater than man, with whom man could establish a personal, intimate contact, should he so will. Such a conception of the Deity does not conflict with the contemporary naturalistic thinking. God is accepted as the immanent reality of the universe, who is *with* all that forms part of nature. He may be viewed as the spiritual dimension of all reality, or the highest single factor within the totality of existence. In the philosophy of Whitehead, the 'consequent nature' of God evolves and develops with the developmental process of the actual world, although Whitehead posits a 'primordial nature' of God too, which like the Absolute of Shankar is the perfect, eternal, ineffable super-reality, identified with the realm of possibility. It is this latter description of a God above God, in the entire speculative venture, that is distasteful to the naturalist. He is reluctant to entertain a theory which conceives God as the designer and planner of the universe, or as its ultimate ground and support.

In *Gurbānī* the supernatural, transcendent aspect of the supreme reality is characterized as the featureless void or *sūnya*, as also the Formless or *Nirañkār* in the ever-abiding state of *Sach-Khand*. In human terms, it is the highest state of spiritual merger of the finite in the infinite,—a unique, extraordinary experience of man's inmost self, not capable of being shared or verified by another. Thus interpreted, the supremely real is, after all, a matter of personal, individual experience. From the naturalist's standpoint, such a view of the 'supreme reality' or its 'realization' issues forth from the metaphysical insight of man; it is a product of his theorizing—an adventure of the human mind, like all other concepts and doctrines, including those concerning the Genesis and cosmic evolution, creativity of God and immortality of the soul. And what originates in the mind and imagination of man, is a *fact* of nature like all facts. Man himself belongs to nature, so do all his concepts and values, as well as his Deity.

The Mystery of Nature and Supernature

According to the Gurus, Truth can be apprehended by the mind, which is the seat of degeneration as well as regeneration of man. The central thesis of their composition stands out as the contemplative grasp of Truth that lifts the individual from a state of delusion to the state of enlightenment. Guru Nanak's *Japujī* itself is Contemplation of Truth : its opening rhyme clinches the issue :

Truth : when nothing else was
Truth : when process of time starts
Truth : what the present sustains
Truth, O Nanak, shall ever remain.[6]

In another context, the Guru builds up a cosmological theory taking Truth as the origin and source of all creation : From Truth arises air, which in turn gives rise to water ; from water are formed the three regions of the universe.[7] The implication that Guru Nanak acknowledged the operation of laws in nature seems unmistakable here. But the Divine Ordinance prevailing in nature is not completely within the human grasp. This is asserted time and again in *Gurbānī*, as for instance :

No measure of the expanse of Thy ordinance is possible;
None can attempt a full account of that.
Even if a hundred poets assemble,
Little would they fathom, coming to grief in the end.
Its true value defies all estimate,
We simply rely on the hearsay.[8]

The state of affairs, symbolically expressed in *Gurbānī* as the 'indescribable description' (*akath kathā*), or the knowability of the unknown, is aptly summed up by the author of the well-known *Chaupaī*, who said :

6 *Ād(i) sach(u) jugād(i) sach(u)* (*Guru Granth*, p. 1)
7 *Sāche te pavanā bhaiā* (*Guru Granth*, p, 19)
8 *Terā hukam(u) na jāpl ketaṛā* (*Guru Granth*, p. 53)

The varying degrees of intellect we have,
Various descriptions we give of Thee, accordingly.[9]

This theme of Truth—and its partial apprehension—is shared by contemporary naturalistic philosophy. The real, essential nature of Truth is hidden from man's view, like a veiled goddess. But the most enigmatic feature of this mystery is that the enigma is soluble. All endeavour of human knowledge is directed to the gradual un-covering of the secrets of both the macrocosmic and the microcosmic aspects of nature. The discovery of the truths proceeds step by step, in a piecemeal fashion, unlike the instant revelation of all secrets claimed by the mystic. The naturalist does not deny the veracity of the holy experience or the divine illumination; nor does he deny the benefits accruing from faith. He himself has a kind of faith, viz. faith in the spirit of inquiry. He treats nature as the home of man, if not of an unknown immaterial spirit.

Traditionally, religion and naturalism have not been friendly to each other. But the modern version of naturalism is no longer an anathema to religion, particularly with its openness to spiritual experience and values that transcend the mundane level of existence. Human life is capable of acquiring ever new meaning, both higher and deeper, which would serve to refashion man's faculties and produce a regenerate individual. If the goal of religion is to transform ordinary beings into idealized souls, the aim of naturalism is no less than the shaping of transfigured men and women. The aesthetic realm of *vismād* or spiritual delight, depicted by Guru Nanak, is the ecstatic realm wherein the mental faculties of man—his vision, intelligence and reason, all are reconstituted into an elevated awareness belonging to sages and seers.[10]

The poets of the *Guru Granth* sing of the mystery that is beyond nature, yet within the bounds of nature. The naturalist is enamoured of the mysterious glory of nature itself—calling to

9 *Ap(u) āpuni budh(i) hai jeti*
Barnat bhin bhin tuh(i) teti (*Dasam Granth*, p. 1387)

10 *Tithai gharīai surat(i) mat(i) man(i) budh(i)*
Tithai gharīai surā sidhā ki sudh(i) (*Guru Granth*, p. 8)

be unveiled at the hands of man. Nature is the common ground between them. It sets limits to the vision of the philosopher of nature, but allows the poetic vision of the seer to pierce through all limits. The naturalist, in measuring up the spiritualist, might discover those features of the order of nature and of the spirit of man—which have inspired mystics and visionaries like the composers of *Gurbānī* to look beyond nature.

5

The Sikh Cosmology

The poetic compositions of the *Adi-Granth* and allied texts are rich in cosmological formulations, even though a consistent, logically worked-out theory of the cosmic order has not been presented in the Sikh scriptures. Religious cosmologies originate from a motive radically different from the one giving rise to cosomological theories in science. In line with the spirit of religious teaching in general, Sikhism attempts to instil faith in the Divine powers, including the power of creation of the universe. The Sikh cosmology, therefore, is part of the speculative venture and spiritual vision of the poet-philosophers whose compositions are enshrined in the holy Granth. Evidently enough, it is not based on any empirical data in the fashion of modern science, nor is it designed to provide explanation of a class of facts, or guidance for future exploration of the origin and nature of the universe as a systematic whole.

The line of demarcation between religion and science in relation to the problem of cosmology, involves the concepts of God and Nature, which, by definition, are exclusive of each other. "If God and Nature are made identical in attributes, both lose their meaning. If God is another name for Nature, then God is not the creator of Nature, for he ceases to have a distinct existence to create Nature." Similarly, "if Nature is another name for God, then Nature is disembodied spiritual existence; for God, by definition, is disembodied spiritual being."[1] In the former case, the whole theological cosmology is rendered meaningless, and in the latter case, physics loses all meaning.

Apart from God and Nature, another concept that is invariably employed in the construction of cosmologies, religious and scientific alike, is the concept of 'creation'. But this concept does not carry the same meaning for the naturalist as it does for the theologian. When the former talks of the 'day of creation', he does not suggest the existence of a spiritual being, or God, performing the function of a creator, at a moment of his choice. Creation here means the coming into existence of the universe as we know it, from the 'embryo' — or the 'cosmic egg'—as it is figuratively called. "How did this 'cosmic egg' appear?" — Science is still unable to answer.[2] Creation, for the man of religion however, is the entirety of the natural world believed to have been established by the divine activity. God is credited with the authorship of the cosmic existence; he may be an entity separate from the created order, as an author is distinct and apart from the work produced by him; but God may also be present in his creation, just as the author is present in his work, and the artist 'lives' in his work of art. No wonder that theologians normally view God as both transcendent and immanent. Sikhism too falls in line on this issue.

The World as Creation

The question of the origin or coming into being of the world appropriately belongs to cosmogony rather than to cosmology, though the issues of both the studies are taken up side by side. "Many primitive cosmogonies and mythologies, the world over, ... see the coming-into-existence of the world as the fruit of the mating of a primeval pair, or as the outcome of the authoritative command of some all-powerful ruler."[3] The Vedic religion of ancient India believed that "the world was fashioned

1 S.P. Kanal, *The Ethics of Devatma*, 1974, p. 36.
2 *Matter & Man*, Peace Publishers Moscow, p. 158.
3 Milton K. Munitz, *The Mystery of Existence*, 1965, p. 202.

from the body of a primitive being, a giant or Purusha, dismembered by the gods." It is however not made clear "whence came this Purusha or these gods themselves?"[4] Some of the Upanishads trace the origin of the world to a 'desire' on the part of the primeval Person, universal Being, or Prajapati, who "got frightened owing to his loneliness" and who "could not rejoice, because one cannot rejoice all alone." "With one-half of himself, he produced a woman, who became his wife; the husband and wife together produced human beings"[5]

The Old Testament gives the story of the Genesis in the well-known passage: "In the beginning God created the heaven and the earth. And the earth was waste and void; and darkness was upon the face of the deep; and the spirit of God moved upon the face of the waters. And God said, Let there be light: and there was light." After creating lands and skies, and man in his own image, within six days, "God rested on the seventh day from all his work which he had made."[6] Here the reference is to a command on the part of God in person. Duncan Greenlees interprets the Sikh cosmogony on similar lines. To the question, "How did this universe come into existence?", he provides the answer — "There was nothing but God; He willed, and out of the Word which expresses that Will the universe is being ceaselessly made."[7] Similarity is about the 'word' or 'command' issuing from the Deity. In the Biblical account, however, the world came into being at one stroke, whereas in Sikhism the universe is shown to be made ceaselessly and without break.

Obviously, the reference to creation through a note sounded by the Creator, in the case of Sikh cosmology, is based upon the expression found in Guru Nanak's Japuji —

> Initiates He the whole process
> from one sound, one Note,
> And million rivers outflow,
> a million forms float. (*Japuji*, G.G.-p.3)

4 A. Barth, *The Religions of India.* 1978 (1881), p. 37.
5 G.S. Ghurye, *Religious Consciousness*, 1955, p. 98.
6 Quoted in *Christian Man*, ed. Norman Ravitch, 1973, p. 6
7 *The Gospel of the Guru Granth Sahib*, Adyar, 1960, p. clxxix.

Perhaps, the symbol of 'one sound' (*eko kavão*) could be interpreted in terms of the Big-Bang theory, which is one of the cosmological models presented by contemporary science. According to this theory, a gigantic explosion splashed large drops of matter in all directions. It was the build-up of energy at the core of the 'cosmic egg' that caused it to explode. "Matter became less concentrated, gravitons and photons began to escape from the clutches of the mighty gravitational field, and streams of intense radiation erupted into the void to herald the birth of the universe in which we are living today and whose mysteries we are probing."[8]

Cosmological Models

Apart from the question of 'origin' of the universe, the cosmological theories made current by men of science, serve as conceptual constructions of the universe, — which is treated as not more than one. All other physical objects, processes or systems of lesser scope are to be regarded as only parts of this all inclusive 'unique' or absolute whole. "To speak of a 'plurality of universes' would be a contradiction, or a misuse of language."[9] Thus scientific cosmology is a study of this whole, or of the large-scale properties of the universe, in order to determine its structure, in accordance with the empirical-rational methods of modern science. In this effort, cosmology discusses and answers a number of philosophical questions, on the basis of its findings brought up to date.

"As science, however, cosmology is powerless to make any inference to a process of creation of the world by a transcendent creator, or to argue for the existence of a Necessary Being " According to Professor Munitz, "Creation should not be thought of as something that took place at some definite mement in the past."[10] Some of the cosmological models present a static picture of the universe. Some others are

8 *Matter & Man*, *op. cit.*, p. 158.
9 Munitz, *op. cit.*, p. 60.
10 *Ibid.*, p. 127.

non-static models, for instance the 'ever-expanding universe' in which the galaxies are receding from one another at enormous velocities. Apart from the Big Bang or Primeval Fireball Theory, proposed in 1927, the other principal theories include the Steady State theory, presented in 1948, according to which there is a process of continuous creation of matter, maintaining the universe in a steady-state of constant density. "There was no beginning to the universe and there will be no end. The universe has always looked more or less the way it does now and it will always look this way."[11] The third major theory is the Oscillating Universe (also called the Pulsating Universe theory), according to which the universe periodically compresses and expands, in alternating phases. Currently it is in the course of an expansion that began with a big bang and is gradually slowing down.

Cosmological theories are not the gift of contemporary science alone. A hundred years ago, Frederick Engels gave fulsome credit to Kant and Laplace for their cosmogony, calculated to reduce a mysterious tangential force to a form of motion thereby doing away with the presupposition of a Creator.[12] He also spoke approvingly of the ancient Greek philosophers who had 'brilliant intuitions', as compared to our strictly scientific research in accordance with observational techniques. In fact, the earliest Greek thinkers were cosmologists, in that they ventured their speculations on the question of the primordial stuff of the world. Whereas the 'first philosopher' Thales said it was 'water', his successors toyed with elements like air, or fire, or with some unspecified, infinite cosmic stuff.

'Water' as the basic material out of which the universe is supposed to have been fashioned, is not peculiar to Western thought. "There are at least two Upanishadic accounts of creation which eschew Brahman, Ātman or Sat as the origin of the cosmos. In one it is water and in the other a spontaneous egg which begins the work of creation." "In the beginning this universe was all water. Water produced the true (*satya*). And Brahman is that 'true'. Brahman produced Prajapati who

11 Brandt & Maran, *New Horizons in Astronomy*, 1972, p. 368.
12 *Dialectics of Nature*, Moscow, 1974, p. 73.

produced the gods. ..." This account is from Brihad-āranyak Upanishad. The other one from Chāndogya Upanishad reads —"In the beginning this world was non-existent (*asat*) and later it became existent (*sat*). It grew and became an egg which lay for a year. At the end of a year it burst open. The two shell-pieces became golden and silvern. The latter is the earth and the former, the golden half, is the sky."[13] The Indian term for the universe is Brahmand (that is, Brahman+und), which means 'cosmic egg'. The term denotes not only the original organic matter inside the egg-shell that became the starting point of it all, but also perhaps the elliptical shape of the egg serving as model for the depiction of the universe, as also of the orbits of the ever-moving planets.

Cosmology in India

India shares with ancient Greek and modern Western thought, another cosmological feature, namely the nebulous or chaotic state from which the universe is supposed to have evolved. The super-explosion or big bang hurled the nebulae apart, giving rise to galaxies and planetary systems. Ancient philosophy refers to an undifferentiated state of Chaos that preceded the formation of the Cosmos; The pre-existing chaotic state was eternally present; it had no temporal beginning like the origin of the space-time world. As pointed out by Barth, the Vedic religion of India had a parallel belief. "It was by sacrifice—it is not said to whom—that the gods delivered the world from chaos...."[14] The mythical element present in the scheme is clearly discernible.

The 'Hymn of Creation' in the Rigveda refers to the pre-cosmic, nebulous state in the following fanciful terms:

> "Non-being then existed not, nor being:
> There was no air, nor sky that is beyond it.
> What was concealed? Wherein ? In whose protection ?
> And was there deep unfathomable water ?

13 Ghurye, *op. cit.*, p. 100.
14 Barth, *op. cit.*, p. 37.

Death then existed not, nor life immortal ;
Of neither night nor day was any token.
By its inherent force the One breathed windless.
No other thing than that beyond existed.

Darkness there was at first by darkness hidden ;
Without distinctive marks, this all was water.
(Macdonell : x, 129)

The hymn further employs concepts like 'desire' and 'creative force' and phrases like 'gods born after this world's creation', and 'none knowing whence creation has arisen'. However, 'darkness' and 'water' stand out as important ingredients of the primal stuff.

On the whole, the Indian tradition assumes the original stuff to be beginningless *(anādi)*, implying that "we do not know what happened long, long ago." According to Devasenapati, "Creation is not a unique event for Hinduism in the sense that it occurs just *once*. Creation is periodic." "As for what happened in the first creation, it is a matter beyond our understanding; it is a mystery."[15] Radhakrishnan, like Whitehead, explains the world process in terms of duality, that is, the Divine interacting with primal matter. "The same duality is indicated in the passage of Genesis relating to the Spirit. ...When the spirit of God brooded on the face of the waters, the original chaos was being shaped into order." "All things in the world participate in the characters of this duality. . . . The world and the World Spirit are both equally real."[16]

The Buddhist cosmology held the entire existence as a flux, a process of 'becoming', on sensual, corporeal and incorporeal planes. In its later development, however, Buddhism propounded "*Sunya-vāda* or Voidism, signifying emptiness and nothingness. *Sunyatā* is the essence of the universe, the root of everything that is, rather the basic unreality of things, and hence renders any positive or logical statement that is made about it

15 *Contemporary Indian Philosophy*, ed. Margaret Chatterjee, 1974, p. 101.
16 Schilpp (Ed.), *The Philosophy of S. Radhakrishnan*, 1952, p. 801.

as superficial." "Nāgārjuna's *sunyatā* is a cipher, indeterminable, unutterable and occult to the entire range of actual and possible knowledge."[17]

To sum up, the Indian position on cosmology works out to this : "Sankhya asserts that the teleology of the *prakriti* is sufficient to explain all order and arrangement of the cosmos. The Mimansakas, the Charvakas, the Buddhists and the Jains all deny the existence of Ishvara (God). Nyaya believes that Ishvara has fashioned this universe by his will out of the ever-existing atoms. . . . This world is not momentary as the Buddhists suppose, but is permanent as atoms, is also an effect so far as it is a collection of atoms, and is made up of parts like all other individual objects."[18]

Cosmology in Guru Nanak Bani

A scientific model in cosmology requires the constant support provided by observational evidence. A philosophical theory appeals to reason; it may interest itself in the empirical data collected by physical science and construct a rationalistic model upon that basis. "Religion has its own insights into the nature of man and the world and it seeks to express them in the form of rational doctrine."[19] Sikhism as a religion presents the intuitive insights of its mentors into reality and its modes, through the medium of poetry. While building up its doctrinal edifice largely on the conceptual foundations provided by India's philosophic heritage, Sikhism rejected the mythical and patently superstitious elements clouding the traditional thinking. In its cosmology, Sikhism tried to do without the tales of a giant dismembered by gods, or the mating of a god-goddess pair. Guru Nanak, however, alludes to these figments of imagination accepted by tradition ; for instance :

The creative Mother in mystery union—
so the tradition holds—

17 Ramakant Sinari, in *Cont. Indian Phil., op. cit.*, pp. 281-2.
18 S.N. Dasgupta, *A History of Indian Philosophy*, 1957. (1922), p. 325.
19 John E. Smith in *Religion* (Princeton), 1965, p. 434.

Brought forth the Dieties three
for carrying on three roles :
One was given Creative powers,
second got Preserver's lot,
Third one to sit in judgment
at the destiny's Court.

(*Japuji*, p. 7)

After stating the traditional position, he puts forth his own thesis that "it is all Divine Will/there is but the only God./He ordains the worldly ways/He performs all the roles."

The depiction of Guru Nanak's pre-cosmic state of the Absolute is remarkably similar to Rigvedic creation-hymn. He talks in terms of the 'trance' of the Formless Spirit, the Absolute Void, the 'power' of Being, its creativity, and potentiality for manifestation and self-revelation.—

In the beginning was inexpressible darkness:
Neither the earth nor sky there was,
The Infinite Will alone prevailed.
Neither day and night
Nor the moon and sun did exist,
The Absolute Void was in eternal stance.
No source of creation, no speech,
No air, no water there were;
No production, no consumption,
No arrival, no departure,
No lands or nether regions,
Not the seven seas
Nor waters flowing down streams. ...

As and when He willed
He brought the world into being
And vaulted heavens without support,
Created He Brahma, Vishnu, Shiva;
And instilled in earthly beings
Sense of attachment over-bearing. ...

Establishing continents, worlds and underworlds,
From state of void unrevealed,
Self-manifest became He. (*Māru Solhe*, p. 1035)

The transition from the hidden (*gupat*) state to the revealed (*pargut*) state was effected through the mysterious 'will' of the Divine, which in the Vedic account has been put down as 'desire'. At any rate, the primordial thought-free (*a-phur*) state was the pre-cosmic state that preceded the thought-full (*sa-phur*) state of names, forms and content, in the Nanak-Bāni.

Again, there is striking resemblance of terminology between the Buddhist Voidism and Guru Nanak's use of equivalent terms implying the void (*sunya*), and unreality (*koor*). However, Guru Nanak invests the concept of Void with 'power' of being; it is *Sunn-kalā*, and not the negation of all creativity, ability and thought. It is not nihilism, or a theory of the cipher or zero. Guru Nanak's *Sunya* or Void is the featureless Spirit that is the ground of the phenomenal world, which again is 'void' when devoid of the spiritual essence. It is for the human mind to experience divine presence in the physical world; without such experience, all existence is crass, non-spirit, physical void. In a hymn on this theme, Guru Nanak says—

The Transcendent Being comes alive
with powers of the absolute Void,
Himself He remains unattached, unaffected,
But goes on creating and viewing Nature;
Out of the featureless Void
he produces the worldly void.
Brahma, Vishnu and Shiva
are born of the Void,
All the ages, temporal order
come out of the Void. ...
Out of the Void came Incarnations ten,
And the universe, with the whole expanse. ...
Of the Void were born the Five Elements,
Producing bodies in concert,
And all practices, all the actions. ...

(*Māru Solhe*, p. 1037)

In Guru Nanak's cosmology, repeated mention is made of water as the supporting element of the cosmic order. Water is the 'father' (*Pāni-Pitā*), which reminds one of the Greek speculation about water as the primal stuff. Water finds mention in Ṛigvedic and Biblical theories of Genesis too. Modern science gives credit to hydrogen for its role in the constitution of the world; and water is two-thirds hydrogen. In one of his compositions, Guru Nanak links water with the three-fold order of creation—

Air arose from Truth Primal,
Out of Air arose the Water;
With water was formed the threefold world
That enshrines the light essential.

(*Sri-Rāga*, p. 19)

The theological position in regard to cosmic creation is clearly asserted in the beginning of Guru Nanak's *Vār Asā*—"The Absolute Spirit created itself/created He the names and forms/ He created Nature as second order/and seated, joyously views it all." The worthy disciple of Guru Nanak and his immediate spiritual successor, Guru Angad Dev, sums up the cosmology and metaphysical outlook of the Master, thus :

This world is the Abode of the holy Lord,
The holy One abides in the world.

(*Vār Asā*, p. 463)

Contribution of Guru Amar Das

Guru Amar Das, as the third Guru, succeeded to the spiritual office of Guru Nanak at the mature age of 73. He was a contemporary of Guru Nanak for 60 years and lived up to the ripe age of 95. In his voluminous compositions, Guru Amar Das enriched the Nanak heritage of enlightened faith, philosophic insight and sublime poetry, with a rare clarity of vision and simplicity of diction. He extended the thought of his predecessors, adding some of the new dimensions to it. His contribution to the Sikh cosmology, in the main, is a confirmation of

Guru Nanak's own cosmological view, emphasizing the divine origin of the world, prevalence of the divine ordinance therein, and the possibility of human realization of the highest truth through the framework of the physical universe and human personality.

The figure of 36-Ages of the pre-cosmic state of void, has been employed by Guru Amar Das (p. 1061), in conformity with the traditional belief in the nine cycles of four great epochs each. Guru Nanak too made a reference to '36 yugas' established by the Transcendent Lord (in *Maru Solhe*). In order to poetically depict the immeasurably long duration of the Absolute Spirit's self-absorption, expressions like innumerable eras of nebulous darkness, and thirty-six ages of divine 'trance' have been used by Guru Nanak and Guru Amar Das.

Again, in conformity with Guru Nanak's conception, Guru Amar Das speaks of the phenomenal world as created by the Lord Supreme (*Oamkār*). "All this wondrous play symbolizes His greatness"—"He makes and remakes the world."—"Like a skilful player, He performs the feat (of creation)." Here, reference is made to the making and remaking of the universe. Elsewhere too, references are found to the repeated cycles of creation and dissolution. It is one of the fundamental tenets of Sikh cosmology that the Divine is not only the creator but also the liquidator of the world. As put by Gopal Singh—"He is the creator and also the destroyer of what He creates. And, then, He re-creates in order to re-destroy."[20] The principle behind this alternation of creation and annihilation seems to be the one stated in the composition *Benati-Chaupai*—

When the Creator projects himself
The world and creatures all take shape;
When He draws in and attracts
All embodiments relapse into Him.

(*Dasam Granth*, p. 1387)

Perhaps it is the same principle of expansion and contraction (*udkarakh* and *ākarakh*) as is at the base of the Pulsating Universe theory. The essential temporality of the phenomenal

20 Gopal Singh, *The Religion of the Sikhs*, 1971, p. 42.

world is a basic assumption of modern cosmologies; all existence, all being is in time; nay, being itself is time. The author of the aforesaid Chaupai had similar vision when he composed :

> In time did Brahma assume a form,
> In time did Shiva come down below;
> In time did Vishnu reveal himself,
> Of time is all this wondrous show.
>
> (*Dasam Granth*, p. 1386)[21]

Another insight of Guru Amar Das relates to the theme of the Formless giving rise to forms. The *Nirankār* is formless, featureless reality, which may be interpreted as the Void; but the whole intent of Gurbāni takes it to be the spiritual Essence without embodiment, which in its blissful freedom takes on the garb of Existence. The Spirit is one; it is unity, though not a blank unity or pure void, since it has the power of self-expression. When revealed, its unity becomes diversity. From the one, unmanifest aspect, it turns into the plural, manifest aspect; then, from the infinity of forms, it returns to its original singularity. From *Anek* (many) it becomes *Ek* (one).[22] Pluralism inherent in the philosophy of existence, turns into monism that characterizes the metaphysics of essence.

A distinctive feature of Guru Amar Das's realistic outlook on life and world, is the stress laid on the physical aspect of things. Numerous of his hymns portray the human body as a treasure of most valuable elements, including the spiritual truths of life. In one composition, he eloquently proclaims the existence of the whole world inside the bodily framework :

> Within the body are contained all entities—
> regions, circles, underworlds;
> Within the body abides the Master—
> of life, world and protector of all.
>
> ... ...

21 English version by S.S. Sekhon.

22 See the *Jaap* of Guru Gobind Singh.

This body is the bearer of Earth,
with nine divisions, stores, bazars. . . .
Within the body are Brahma, Vishnu, Shiva,
and the entire universe He produces;
The holy Lord has established his Play—
with process of ceaseless coming and going. ...

(*Suhi*, p. 754)

Guru Amar Das is one with Guru Nanak and his successors on the ultimate creative powers residing in the Primordial Person (*Adi Purakh*). According to Guru Nanak, "The Lord is engaged in the endless process of creation" —(*Tukhāri Bārāmāha*, p. 1007); "the creation and dissolution are the work of the everlasting Divine, and of none else"—(*Rāmkali*, p. 905). Guru Amar Das readily supports this contention—"Creation and annihilation occur through the Word; out of the Word rises the world again and again"—(*Mājh*, p. 117). The same article of faith holds good for Guru Arjan too—

Real Himself, real is all He makes;
The whole creation from the Divine emanates;
If He so wills, expansion initiates;
If He so wills, all in One concentrates.

(*Sukhmani*, p. 294)

A major conclusion that emerges from the foregoing is in regard to the concept of 'continual creation' at the hands of God. Fred Hoyle emphasizes the need of such a principle, without however invoking the agency of God. Says he—"Without continuous creation the universe must evolve towards a dead state in which all the matter is condensed into a vast number of dead stars. ... With continuous creation the universe has an infinite future in which all its present very large-scale features will be preserved." "I think that of all the various possibilities that have been suggested, continuous creation is easily the most satisfactory."[23]

23 Quoted in *The Changing Concepts of the Universe* (A.M.U. Aligarh), 1963, pp. 104-8.

Mysteries of Creation

The subject of cosmology, be it in the hands of philosophers and scientists, or be it with spiritual visionaries like Guru Nanak and his successors, finds itself surrounded by some of the unresolved mysteries. Is the universe finite or infinite, bounded or unbounded? At one time, Einstein himself pictured it as a finite and unbounded universe, though in the light of his own discoveries, this hypothesis was abandoned in favour of a model suggesting infinity of the cosmic creation. As put by Hoyle—"One of the questions we shall have to consider later is what lies beyond the range of our most powerful instruments. But even within the range of observation there are about 100,000,000 galaxies. With upward of 1,000,000 planetary systems per galaxy the combined total for the parts of the universe that we can see comes out more than a hundred million million."[24] Guru Nanak's answer is not far different—

> Millions are the underworlds,
> millions float in space;
> Despairing of the final count
> Vedas give up stake.
>
> (*Japuji*, p. 5.)

The mystery of the extent of creation is nowhere claimed to have been solved or comprehended in full measure in Gurbāni. And what the distances are like, traversed by the celestial bodies?—

> In control moves the sun,
> in discipline moves the moon;
> Billions of miles they travel,
> with no halt, no end.
>
> (*Vār Asā*, p. 464)

Indian thinkers of antiquity and scientists of today, both talk in terms of the 'cosmic egg'—without solving the puzzle of its

24 *Ibid.*, p. 95.

origin. Who laid that 'egg'? And when? In terms of the temporal order, can anyone pin-point the 'day of creation'? And since the phases of expansion and contraction are beyond count or estimation, how can one speak of the 'first' creation? "As regards the beginning," says Guru Nanak, "the best course is to admit to a sense of wonderfulness"—that is, ecstasy or *vismāda*, since "the featureless Void was in ceaseless existence"—(*Sidha Goshti*, p. 940). On the issue of the time of creation, Guru Nanak's view expressed in the Japuji is quite well known—

> What the hour, what the time,
> what date and day?
> Which the season, which month
> when came the cosmic Play?
> Knew not the Pundits time,
> though given a hint in Purān;
> Knew not the Qazis time—
> who composed the Qurān.
> Nor knows the yogi time—
> season, month or dates:
> He-himself the secret knows,
> who the world creates.
>
> (*Japuji* p. 4)

In our times, Dr. Radhakrishnan has echoed this view by proclaiming that the meaning of mystery, the origin of the world, cannot be scientifically apprehended. Says he—"Within the temporal process itself, science offers explanations for particular events, but it cannot deal with the why of the temporal process as a whole." Expressing his faith in the 'absolute freedom' of the Absolute Being, he adds: "The mystery of the world abides in freedom. Freedom is the primordial source and condition of all existence. It precedes all determination."[25]

Then, there is the mystery of the reality or unreality of the created world. Radhakrishnan so interprets the Advaitic doctrine of Māyā, as to save the world and give to it a real meaning.

25 Schilpp, *op. cit.*, pp. 38-40.

For one thing, he considers the essential temporality of the world as *māyā*, without reducing the world into an illusion. Again, the creative power of the Divine and the mysterious working of his will, are to be treated as *māyā*. Finally, "Māyā is also used for ignorance by which we do not recognise the principle of the universe."[26] Man's non-knowing or *avidyā* is the meaning he gives to the term, that comes closest to the Sikh doctrine of Māyā. Guru Arjan's enunciation that a Real World proceeds from the Real Being, is anticipated in Guru Nanak's enunciation—

Real are the regions Thine,
real the universes,
Real are spheres Thine,
real the forms created.

(*Vār Asā*, p. 463)

But, if the entire creation is real, then why does Guru Nanak apply the epithet of *koor* or unreality to it ? How is it that Guru Amar Das calls this world an earthen structure or *mitti kā putlā* ? In what sense Guru Tegh Bahadur views the world as a mount of smoke ? The answer lies in human ignorance that mistakes the contingent for the necessary, temporal for the eternal. Man, in his *avidyā*, looks at the creation without realizing the Creator; he views the *qudrat* but not its Qādir; he is aware of existence, but not of essence. Sikhism holds the created world-order as real, unless delusion makes men overlook the divine principle of its creation.

Cosmic Order & Essence

One of the questions philosophy considers in the course of its cosmological ventures, pertains to the possible relationship obtaining between the cosmic order as Existence and the postulated creative spirit as Essence. In theological language, the question centres on the relation of God to man's world. Admitting that the relationship (as between the author and his

26 *Ibid.*, p. 801.

product) does obtain, a further question arises regarding the multiplicity of such creation. Can we claim, in the context of Sikh cosmology, that this is a two-way relation ? "For Whitehead there is a mutual relationship (not symmetrical in every respect) between God and the world. God exhibits primary action on the world, but there is also a reaction of the world on God." "God is not only *with* the world at the beginning (primordial nature) but he is also the end (consequent nature) and, as such, he shares in the novel elements resulting from the ongoing cosmic process in time. ... One of the principal consequences of this doctrine is that there is an 'advance' in God."[27]

Sikh cosmology would scarcely entertain the idea of the created world-order effecting any change in the already accomplished nature of the Creator-Divine Person (Kartā-Purakh). However, it may readily accept the contention that the creatures can and do persuade the benign Creator to bestow his blessings upon them. The doctrine of Grace fits in with the whole scheme. Secondly, the natural world is believed to be governed by the Divine Ordinance (*Hukam*). "Philosophically, *Hukam* is the apprehension of that mystery which underlies all existence, and which can express itself only in the action of submission and resignation."[28]

The conclusion thus emerges that in Sikhism the finite can to some extent influencc the Infinite, through devotion and resignation, even if the essential nature of the perfect God is not affected. The problem, however, does not end here. Man as a finite and temporal creature tries in his finite ways to apprehend what is infinite and eternal. Einstein once wrote, without laying claim to comprehensiveness of his investigations, that "it was hardly reasonable to extend the laws of finite matter to the infinite universe."[29] How can man, as a part of the space-time order or Existence, claim to know what transcends this order and whose Being is interpreted in terms of pure Essence ?

According to Guru Amar Das, "the Divine creates the world and keeps it within his control"—(*Vār Gujri*, p. 517). If so,

27 John E. Smith, *op. cit.* pp. 436-7.
28 G.S. Talib, *Guru Nanak*, 1969, p. 147.
29 *Matter & Man*, *op. cit.* p. 166.

then man is not free to exercise control over the Creator; at best he can understand the motions of the Master to an extent the latter permits him to do. Moreover, the appearance of the world is associated with the egoistic sense of the individual. To the question of the Sidhas as to how the world arises, Guru Nanak replied that "the world arises in the ego"—meaning thereby that the phenomenal world, though not a creation of man, appears in the consciousness of wordly beings including man. And the very spirit that is immanent in the universe (*Brahmand*), is to be found inside the body (*pind*). The Divine Essence is present, not only in the macrocosm, but also in the microcosm. In this way, human experience, the world, and God are linked to one another.

The Sikh cosmology, based on a profound theistic faith, finally eliminates the duality of Nature and God, existence and essence, through a formula that brings the Essence within the ambit of Existence. Guru Nanak perceives the same Light everywhere and in every heart; for him one single Essence pervades and informs the entire multiplicity of the cosmic existence. It is not a case of Essence and Existence, but simply a case of Essence-in-Existence.[30] And Guru Amar Das exhorts man to realize the same Essence in oneself:

> You embody the very Light, O Man,
> Recognize the Essence of your life.
>
> (*Asā*, p. 441)

30 Cf. Wazir Singh, *Humanism of Guru Nanak*, 1977, pp. 161-4.

6

Ethical Orientation of Sikhism

Let there be a community of virtues,
Let the vices be abandoned. — Guru Nanak, *Suhi*

There is a fundamental community between religion and morality, namely the common objective of human excellence. The spiritual message of religion carves out the path of faith and belief for the welfare of human beings. It inspires the individual to release himself from the bondage of his own ego, and to develop cosmic awareness and divine vision. The path of morality is the path of conscious action and self-reliance. It provides the individual with orientation of the values of human life, and fortifies him with the inspiration to rise above his personal interests in order to actively serve the common interests of mankind. Religious instruction and ethical teaching both become instrumental in the transformation of the individual and collective human life into a richer, more meaningful and rewarding life.

Religion has to adopt, for the fulfilment of its objective, moral and ethical means. Rare indeed would be a religious faith in the world which fails to prescribe a set of ethical principles for the evolution of spiritual life. On the other hand, instances may be cited of ethical systems functioning independently of theism or a spiritualistic base, as in the case of Buddhism. In Sikhism, however, a synthesis of spiritual and ethical aspects is available. Gurbāni (the spiritual compositions of

Sikhism) indicates, primarily, a highway for the atttainment of divine experience. Such an experience is purely spiritual and non-moral; but the means that the individual has to choose for promoting this ideal, are intimately concerned with the performance of moral action. The highest value of Sikh ethics is indeed a value of the spiritual order, but the moral values that aid in the attainment of this value are also helpful in raising the quality of an individual's life to a higher social and cultural plane. The re-structured mental faculties of awareness and intellect, and consciousness of the level of sages and savants, not only put the spiritual seeker on the path leading to the realms of Creativity and Nobility, but also mould him into a person of exquisite making, wide vision and excellent virtues,—who is but a significant and fully reformed member of the human community.

Man's duties, his moral virtues, and his ideals and values are foremost among the problems of ethics. What is the obligation of the individual and how is it related to the ethical ideal? Should the individual practise moral virtues with a view to attaining some objective, or ought he to exercise his moral obligation without expecting a reward? Gurbāni attaches importance to the motive-free action, so far as purely moral life is concerned; the individual ought to give priority to the virtuous act irrespective of personal gain or selfish aim.[1] However, in the sphere of spiritual attainment, the moral action presents itself only as a means to the chosen end. Without inculcation of ethical virtues, devotion to God is not possible either. Is the primary and fundamental orientation of Gurbāni ethical or spiritual?—Although a final and decisive answer to this question is difficult to offer, the spirit of Gurbāni, on the whole, is indicative of the primacy given to a mystical, spiritual experience, even as the scriptural compositions are not found wanting in elements and expressions of ethical import.

The Ideal Man of Gurbani

The individual recognized by the spiritualistic tradition of

1 In performance of action shall he be free of motive,...
He shall not aim at the fruit of action. (*Sukhmani*, 5)

Gurbāni as 'ideal person', is often designated as 'Gurmukh' and 'Brahmn-Gyāni.' Such a one has also been given the epithets of sage (*sādh-jan*), saint, *pancha* or *pradhān*; his most prominent trait is the state of emancipation-in-life (*jivan-mukti*). He adopts a way of life that, on one hand, opens up the door to inner awareness, and on the other motivates the seeker for the performance of good actions. This way of life is replete with overwhelming desire to forge ahead, with no inclination to turn backwards.[2] According to Guru Amar Das—

> The God-oriented ones are never senile,
> Within they carry wisdom divine. (*Sloka*)

The *gurmukhs* trade in holy commerce. For them, the gist of ethical virtues consists in the following:

> For whom the discipline is of Truth,
> The holy sport of Contentment,
> The ablution of Wisdom and Meditation,
> With compassion their idol, forgiveness their rosary—
> Such indeed are the elect ones. (*Vār Sārang*, Guru Nanak)

In the Indian tradition, Buddhism is known to have presented the ideal of *boddhisattva*, and the Bhagvad Gita the ideal of *sthitapragya*. The individual attaining to the status of *boddhisattva* comes to have an insight into the reality of the world; he acquires awareness of the highest truth; transcending his individuality, he prepares himself for eradicating the anguish and suffering of mankind. The ideal man of the Gita is possessed of equipoise and balanced intellect. He is directed and guided by the virtues he carries within; he is in a position to cognize and carry out his obligation. In line with this tradition, the Gurmukh and Brahmn-gyāni of Sikhism is the ideal man of spiritual insight and ethical disposition; but he is, at the same time, a devotee of the Lord, imbued with love for Him, and capable of enjoying the mysteries divine. Knowledge and vision of God may be the highest attainment of human intellect, but the inner

2 Keep marching forward, turn not the shoulder back. (*Vār Māru, 5*)

experience of God, to enjoy God and live through Him, would be the climax of aesthetic disposition. The ideal man of Gu bāni is the knowledgeable and virtuous soul, capable of enjoying the Lord. He has developed a vision that is at once unique and beatific.

The ethical principles, values and obligations that have found exposition in Gurbāni, presented as they are through the medium of poetry, are not to be found in any definitive logical pattern or order, but are free expressions of the poetic minds. One has to glean ethical elements from Gurbāni and place them in a system, classification or framework, according to one's light.

The Highest Values of Gurbani

Every religious tradition presents man with a selection of ideals which serve the concerned community and its members as the exalted values. Likewise, certain schools of contemporary philosophy find fulfilment of their elected task, in providing an orientation of values to man. From this angle, existentialism comes quite close to the spirit of religion; it has accorded priority to the establishing of a system of human values, instead of giving preference to the traditional metaphysical issues of philosophy. And like Buddhism, it has sought ways and means of eliminating suffering and anguish of man. It is with this spirit of human welfare that a close community of the objectives of Gurbāni may be found. The latter has furnished man with an orientation of values that serve as goals of human life, even though the Sikh philosophy also offers a system of values that may well be the attributes of the Absolute, rather than being possible objects of human realization, as for instance the divine attributes of infinity, eternality, universal immanence etc.

So far as human values are concerned, at least five intrinsic values find mention in Gurbāni, which of course may be treated as the highest values of the Sikh faith.

(1) *The secret of alphabet.*— This is the value of the light of learning, of enlightenment, the promotion of which brings the glow of wisdom in one's life. Kabir refers to this value thus:

Let us acquire a measure of knowledge
To instruct and guide the mind. (*Bāvan Akhari*)

Granted that Gurbāni does not recognize mere reading-and-writing as of any special merit in itself: "The individual who meditates on the Lord, realizes the supreme goal, be he lettered or unlettered."—(*Gauri* 5). And if formal education leads not to the eradication of one's egoistic hankerings, what use is it to read through piles upon piles of books? Yet, Gurbāni accords an exalted place to learning and enlightenment. Those who are devoid of all awareness of the essence of existence and life, those altogether deprived of intellectual endowment, those unable to decipher even 'letters of alphabet'—are no better than the ass, according to Guru Nanak.[3] Intelligence is required even for prayer and meditation; intelligent activity leads one to the call of honour.[4] "Says Nanak—Let us hear a bit and speak a bit, as long as we stay put."—(*Dhanāsri*). But this much of discrimination is necessary, as says Kabir—"Have discourse with a saintly fellow you meet; meeting with a depraved one, better keep mum."—(*Gond*).

Knowledge of the secret of alphabet is considered essential for having an insight into the vastness of the universe; for "the Lord has created the three regions of existence through the Word." And "the entire phenomenal existence is but the sound of Letter."—(*Bāvan Akhri*, 5). In the Japuji is a mention of "meditation through the letters, praise through the words." In the *Rāmkali Onkār* is a reference to "the account of existence through letters and words." Without acquisition of a sense of language, how can one hope to follow the teachings of scriptures and to cleanse the mind of sinful disposition?

As the lamp is lit, darkness vanishes,
Learning of holy teaching washes away the sins.
When the sun rises, the moon seems not,
When knowledge sheds light, ignorance is gone.
(*Vār Suhi*, Guru Nanak)

3 Cf. *Vār Sārang*.
4 Ibid.

According to Saint Kabir, the wind of wisdom blows away all delusion and illusion.[5] A wide-awake, thoughtful and conscientious person is capable of inculcating ethical qualities as well. Sheikh Farid scarcely expects a 'fine intellect' to indulge in slander.

Guru Amar Das, in considering the traits of a knowledgeable personality, asserts—"The wise one is wide-awake; in darkness stalks the ignorant one."—(*Vār Bihāgrā*). And "To the wise is revealed all truth; all truth is known to them."—(*Asā*). The 'knower' is one that discovers the secret of reality inside his own self—"Pondering one's inner being makes for the wise one."—(*Gauri*). And, where there is enlightenment, there is righteousness, where there is falsehood, there is sin.[6] What could be more concise and complete a definition of altruism, than the dictum—

"A benefactor is one
Who truly contemplates learning"? (*Asā*, G.N.)

But, if the deciphering of alphabet leaves the conduct unaffected and unreformed, education is in vain. "Speak not evil to anyone : that is the lesson of learning ; involve not yourself with a fool "—(*Vār Asā*, 1).

(2) *Humanism.*—The humanism of Gurbāni is indicative of love for the Divine, on one hand, and love for humanity and welfare of all, on the other. In humanity too the light of the Lord is immanent.[7] The entire cosmos is the outcome of that divine glow. Whom are we to treat as good, and whom evil?[8] Such a humanism does not regard man as the centre or pivot of cosmic creation, even though it may accept his overlordship on the earth. Gurbāni offers a synthesis of humanism and

5 Cf. *Gauri*, Kabir.
6 Cf. *Sloka*, Kabir.
7 All souls shine with that very light,
The Light Divine lights up everyone's being. —(*Dhanāsri, 1*)
8 The Transcendent Lord at first, created the primal light;
from nature emanate all the things,
The entire world came from the same source;
how then is anyone good or bad? —(*Prabhāti*, Kabir)

theism. Love of God may be instrumental in the envisagement of God in humanity, in the loving of human beings. Love of humanity may serve as a means to the love of God immanent in all human hearts. It is through reverence of humanity, through service and benevolence, through compassion and justice that love of human beings becomes possible. It may take another form as the mutual love of wife and husband, which is made a symbol of the mystic love for the Lord in Gurbāni. Baba Farid talks of "letting the youthful charm slip away, if the love of my darling be maintained." Here the darling is husband that symbolizes man and God both. All activity, ritual or custom that alienates the beloved from her Lord or makes her forget Him, is worthless[9] The devotee of the Lord is his worshipper and lover ; the Lord resides in his heart; he perceives the Master in all the creatures. The devotee's humanism inspires him to work for the welfare of human beings; its spirit lies in directing the lost and misled ones on to the right path, to the path of God's love. The light that has demonstrated to him the being of his beloved Lord, appears to him as immanent in all forms of life :

His light is present in all species,
He is experienced in that Light.
Free of attributes, yet attributes all He assumes.
—(*Asā*, G.N.)

All belong to the Commune Divine,
To none Thou appeareth alien. —(*Mājh*, 5)

(3) *Ecstasy.*—Following the intellectual and humanistic values, it is now the turn to determine the aesthetic value in Gurbāni. This is the value of the balanced state of the human mind, for which symbols like *sehaj* (equipoise), *anand* (bliss), *vismād* (wonderment) have been employed. This state may result from the ecstasy of the meditation of Nām, from treading the path of spiritual awareness, realizing the one absolute Truth inside and

9 Let the custom that separates me from my Lord, be burnt.
—(*Vad-hans Vār*, 1)

outside, and absorbing oneself in it. When the vision of the Creator's 'true' Creation impresses one all around, the longing to merge into the creator residing in nature gets firmer. The colourful variety and expanse of Nature and its wondrous grandeur give rise to ecstatic state of wonderfulness,—"perceiving the grandiose phenomena, with wonderment am I struck."—(*Asā*,1). When the individual examines his body and being, when he has an insight into the inmost of his mind and finds the light of that very Spirit present, when he recognizes his own 'essence', he gets the experience of ecstatic wonderment. His balanced vision obtains a uniform view of the light within, and of Nature's objects and forms without. It is in such a state of equipoise that all anguish and suffering vanish, the stage of Nirvāna is acquired, and the mystical awareness brings forth an experience of absolute blissfulness.[10]

(4) *Absolute Consciousness.*—Mystery of the Spirit, of which the individual's aesthetic sense produces a beatific state of ecstasy, the intuitional vision of the same mystery furnishes one with the highest knowledge, which the text of Gurbāni names *Brahmn-Gyān* (absolute consciousness). If we take this state in the intellectual sense of 'cosmic consciousness'—it amounts to resplendent knowledge of universal laws operating in the world, of the countless Indras, moon and suns, of numerous regions and counties ; if we look at it in the sense of a description of the Indescribable, fulness of attributes of the Attributeless, qualitative aspect of the qualityless Void wrapt in-itself, it comes to mean a vision of the Absolute Spirit, or knowledge of Brahman. Gurbāni often assigns the symbol of Veda to absolute consciousness. The Sukhmani and other texts offer detailed account of the characteristics of a *Brahmn-gyāni*. To the knowing individual endowed with intuitive insight, the secret of "drop in the ocean and ocean in the drop" opens up. The gist of the balanced vision of such a one consists in this—

The female is immanent in the male,
The male is present in the female—
To Brahmn-gyāni is the mystery revealed. —(*Rāmkali*,G.N.)

10 Contemplation of the Word of Enlightener brings the final joy.
—(*Asā*, 5)

Be it the ecstatic state of beatific joy, or be it the ever wakeful state of absolute consciousness, in terms of Gurbāni it is not merely a stage of individualistic or personal achievements; rather—

Brahmn-gyāni is vehemently disposed
to acts of benevolence. —(*Sukhmani*, 5)

From the standpoint of Brahmn-gyāni's vision of equanimity and composure, "none is an enemy, none the alien." Such a one is 'ever non-attached' and 'never evil-doing'. Fearlessness is an inseparable characteristic of his being :

He is the one who suffers not in suffering,
Cares not for comfort or pleasure,
And knows no fear,
Gold and dust he treats equally. —(*Sorath*, 9)

(5) *Emancipation-in-life.*—In terms of Gurbani's ideology, the state of emancipation-in-life may be regarded as the highest value and ideal of human life. Blissful ecstasy and absolute consciousness cannot be separated from this state. The individual who is liberated in life seeks nothing for his personal benefit, not even *mukti* or salvation,—he longs only to be worthy of Lord's love—

I seek not reign or rule,
I covet not salvation for the soul,
Love of the 'lotus feet' of Lord
do I seek alone. —(*Dev Gandhāri*, 5)

He has ended his sense of individuality, self-pride, and egoism—

The emancipated-in-life is one
Who does away with ego inside. —(*Māru*, G.N.)

From his point of view—

Pleasure and pain affect him not,
Foe and friend are alike.

—(*Sloka*, 9)

He has discovered a way of life that makes it possible to attain salvation even while one is engaged in playing and enjoying oneself, in eating and drinking, and dressing oneself,—and this very course is the ideal way of life, according to Gurbāni. This is not the ideal of spiritual peace attainable after death; this is the consummate style of life that comprises the light of learning, the moulding of a humanistic disposition, and abandoning of egoism, —a way of life coloured with loving devotion. It is not different from a state of life tempered with truthfulness,—an unmistakable sign of which is stated by Sheikh Farid :

Those alone are truthful indeed
Who bear love in their hearts. —(*Asā*)

And— Truth is known and realized
When the True One lives in the heart. —(*Vār Asā*, G.N.)

The State of *jivan-mukti* is the state of merger of the individual and the Divine. Both are harmonized into one. Gurbāni has assigned the symbol of *Naad* (symphony) to this state, just as the symbol of Veda is given to Brahmn-gyān. The *anahat-naad* (unstruck melody) of the Yogic cult has assumed the form of harmonious merger of the self with the ultimate Spirit.

The Cardinal Virtues

Besides determining the highest values of spiritual life, Gurbāni lays down the chief virtues of a moral life. Virtues stand for the qualities of a life of goodness or moral excellence, the practice of which is considered essential for the formation of an ideal society.

(1) *Aesthetic discrimination.*—Gurbāni administers warning against engrossing oneself in the sensuous pleasures of the world, but it admits aesthetic discrimination as a trait of the sensible individual.[11] The absence of a sense for music is absence of aesthetic sensibility. According to Gurbāni, "*kirtan* is an invaluable gem." And without the joy derived from meditation, "leading of life in the world is a curse." The aesthetically inclined person is inspired by Gurbāni to adopt higher and nobler tastes:

The love-lorn devotee in absorption
Drinks the nectar of God's name;
Humbug are all other joys for him.
... ...
Damsels numerous, beauty enchanting,
All are joyless, before the joy of meditation. —(*Asā*, 5)

(2) *Contentment.*—For the excellence of an individual life, the virtue of contentment seems indispensable; its application serves to develop humanitarian disposition in the individual. Service is a social act that, in terms of Gurbāni, the 'contented souls' alone can perform. They do not tread the path of evil; they are satisfied with the frugal intake of food and drink. One who practises contentment, prefers "taking all the sufferings like nectar" to a life of dishonour, for—

If one lives with honour lost,
Unworthy is all what he eats. —(*Vār Mājh*, G.N.)

(3) *Conduct truthful.*—According to Gurbāni, a practical life of truthfulness, fidelity, self-control and purity, is higher than the metaphysical Truth.[12] This is a virtue of truthful discipline and principled conduct—

The true bliss comes from truthful acts. —(*Prabhāti*, G.N.)

11 Cf. *Vār Sārang* of Guru Nanak.
12 All else falls short of Truth, yet higher than truth is conduct truthful. —(*Sri Rāg*, 1)

(4) *Effort.*—Gurbāni does not advocate a form of effort or activity that leads man to take pride in his own power and to disregard the potentialities of the Divine power. As an ethical virtue, effort provides the inspiration to "accomplish one's task through one's own labour." This is a homily to the individual to "lead a life of effort and activity, and to enjoy oneself in earning one's livelihood." He who exercises the virtue of effort, need not "lead a life of dependence."

(5) *Fearlessness.*—Ethical theories, both classical and modern, have placed fortitude, valiance or fearlessness among the lists of cardinal virtues. Bringing into being the fearless individual and fearless community has been the dream of serious thinkers. Guru Tegh Bahadur tells the merit of a person possessed of wisdom, thus—

Nôt to frighten anyone,
Nor to be afraid !
O my mind, listen—
Such a one is wise indeed. —(*Slokas*)

Pursuit and attainment of fearlessness consists in the search for and acquisition of the truth—

Man, on begetting Truth, leaves all fear. —(*Sri Rāg*, G.N.)

(6) *Forgiveness-Compassion.*—The social and humanistic spirit of Gurbāni becomes amply clear from the advocacy of the virtues of forgiveness and compassion. Guru Nanak asked for the sacred cord made of the cotton of 'compassion'. According to Baba Farid, a *bhakta* or devotee is the one imbued with a spirit of sacrifice, one who "shares even when dispossessed." The spirit of welfare of all is evident in the assertion:

Contentment in mind, compassion for all
Lead to perfection of righteous life. —(*Gauri*, 5)

(7) *Humility.*—"The sweet modesty, O Nanak, is the essence of virtuous qualities,"—through this dictum, Guru Nanak praises the individual blessed with sweet disposition and speech.

With the help of education and acquisition of learning, the virtue of "speaking not ill to anyone" is developed. Sheikh Farid is emphatically direct in enjoining us—

Utter not words that hurt,
The True Lord resides in all beings. —(*S!okas*)

Criticism of indecent and rude speech is available in *Vār Asā* too: "By uttering indecent words, our body and mind too are fouled." So much so, that "the rude ones are condemned in the Divine Court; their faces get defiled." The essence of the virtue of modesty is this—

Wherever we may be
Let us utter decent words. —(*Vad-hans*, G.N.)

(9) *Non-attachment.*—The way of life that prescribes the course of salvation through enjoying and playing, eating and dressing, includes the commandment of non-attachment, by alluding to the "lotus flower remaining dry and detached while floating on the water." No doubt, Gurbāni warns man against indulgence in the pleasures and comforts of worldly life, but it does not advise escape from or renunciation of the day-to-day life. Gurbāni commends the virtue of non-attachment, not renunciation.

(9) *Temperance.*—The control of a well-groomed life-style over the desires, greed and passions of wordly life, is the virtue of temperance. According to Guru Amar Das—"Ignorance and craving burn away the being of man."—(*Māru*). And—"Be it young or be it aged, the self-oriented are not free from craving and hunger."—(*Sorath*). A stern castigation of a life without moderation is available in these words—

Cursed be the life that is led
Only to eat and swell the belly. —(*Vār Suhi*, G.N.)

(10) *Wisdom.*—Gurbāni accords a place of honour to thoughtful and rational disposition, and intellection. The anvil of 'intelligence' and apparatus of 'wise learning'—are parts of

the holy mint. Among the listing of virtues of "truthfulness, contentment, wisdom," and "self-discipline, contentment, ratiocination," the significance of intellectual virtues of knowledge and wisdom is quite evident. The discipline of 'higher intellect' over the passion-ridden mind is necessary, since "the mind is held in place through consciousness divine." This is not knowledge in the sense of frisking of the mind or clever devices; this is a synthesis of wisdom and truthful conduct not found easily—

Rare in the world is a knowing soul with conduct right,
Rare is the pundit with wisdom high. —(*Asā*, G.N.)

The awakened soul ponders essence. —(*Bhairon*, 3)

Ethical Commands and Duties

Human beings have to perform certain sets of duties in order to pursue ideals and identify virtues. Gurbāni has repeatedly drawn attention to moral obligations and, directly or indirectly, issued commandments, sticking to which man may promote the values set before him. Two fundamental imperatives are (a) recognition of Divine Ordinance, and (b) control over egoism. As regards the sense of ego, Gurbāni has a definite outlook—

Man is placed under the affliction of egoism.
—(*Bhairon*, 5)

So: Give up the sense of ego, O man,
Removing ego, contemplate
And welcome virtues alone. —(*Basant*, G.N.)

Similarly: Truth is not attained by asserting ego or 'I'—
Removing sense of ego, realize status high.
—(*Gauri*, G.N.)

Gurbāni completely rejects the ideology that advocates

development of *khudi* or sense of individuation. The latter requires to be eliminated—

When *khudi* is no more, joy descends—
Mind and body regain health. —(*Bāvan-Akhri*, 5)

The remedy for the malady of egoism is surely indicated in Gurbāni—

He who recognizes the Ordinance, Nanak,
Never shall assert his ego again. —(*Japuji*)

Guru Nanak has given the imperative of resigning oneself to the Divine Will. The ideal man of Gurbāni is the seeker of Divine Ordinance pervading the universe,—one who finds the Ordinance as his Lord's will.

Another commandment so often repeated in Gurbāni is to renounce lust, wrath, covetousness, infatuation and pride. These five evils flourish on the affliction that is egoism. Their cure lies in banishing the direction given by passions and bringing the mind in tune with the Enlightener's teaching.[13] The mind ought to be kept in trimmed-up state—

What use it is, Kabir, to keep the head neatly shorn,
When the mind is not well-trimmed?
All that is done, is by the mind,
Trimming and shearing go in waste. —(*Slokas*, Kabir)

Guru Nanak issued a concise and pithy command in regard to hypocrisy and pretence—"Abandon hypocrisy!" —(*Vār Asā*)

Saint Kabir graphically depicts the hypocritical 'holy' men:

Donning three-and-half yards of *dhotis*,
They wear sacred threads three-fold;

13 Cf. *Bilāval*, 5.

Around their necks rosaries they have,
In hands, begging bowls bright.
Call them not the fellows of God,
Thugs of Benāras are they sure. —(*Asā, Kabir*)

If the mind is defiled with the filth of evils, release from hypocrisy becomes difficult.[14] Nor do the holy dips at *tirthas* remove the dirt, if the mind is full of deceit, and the body engaged in stealth: "Outside the skin is washed bright, but inside is the poison pure." As against such hypocritical ablutions,—

Saints are better even without wash,
A thief is but a thief, howsoever soaked.
—(*Vār Suhi*, G N.)

Human nature is so framed that man is slack and slothful in doing goodness, but he jumps at evil deeds 'like a tiger'.[15] That is why Gurbāni lays stress on the exercise of virtue, on practice:

Let the thoughtful consider, says Nanak—
It is action that matters in the world. —(*Sorath*, G.N.)

And, "Wherever is action, there follows wholesome thought." —(*Sri Rāg*, 1). Without the practice of moral deeds, spiritual attainment is not possible.[16] Nor can the acts be separated from the consequences that flow therefrom:

As are the deeds, so is the man. —(*Suhi*, G.N.)

Fruit follows the quality of our deeds. —(*Vār Asā*, 1)

A straight and simple imperative of Sheikh Farid serves as a pointer to the excellence of ethical life—

14 Cf. *Sorath*, 1.
15 Cf. *Vār Gujri*, 5.
16 Cf. *Gauri*, 5.

Farid, do good unto the evil-doer,
Nurse not anger in the mind. —(*Slokas*)

For making a choice out of virtues and vices, Baba Farid's directive is positive enough—"Farid, give up the acts that bear not goodness." People cling to the evil deeds, but fight shy of good acts.[17] Gurbāni insists on one's becoming a "customer of virtue." Indecisiveness, self-delusion, clever devices—all are evils: the right course is to fight them off.[18] As for virtues, it is proper to make them a common concern.[19] Virtues alone lead to the realization of joy divine—

Holy words purify man,
Virtues bring forth spiritual peace. —(*Asā*, 3)

As long as mental filth persists, how can the individual claim to be 'pure'?[20] And, who is the pure one?—

He is pure who conquers wrath,
Follows divine words and reforms himself. —(*Māru*, 3)

Some other commands are as follows:

Company: Keep not company with the vicious,
Let us shun them from afar.
—(*Slokas*, Kabir)

Compassion: Cause not suffering to anyone,
With honour return to thy Home.
—(*Vār Gauri*, 5)

Contemplation: Listen O pundit, virtuous one,
Perform the act that leads to joy,
And contemplate the essence spiritual.
—(*Sorath*, 1)

17 Cf. *Māru Vār*, 3.
18 Cf. *Gauri*, 5.
19 Cf. *Suhi*, 1.
20 Cf. *Dhanāsari*, 1; *Vad-hans*, 3.

High and Low:	Treat everyone as high, Look down upon none as low. —(*Sri Rāg*, G.N.)
Labour:	Earn through thy labour honest, And set apart a share for others. —(*Vār Sārang*, 1)
Pride/Conceit:	Why entertain pride, When we live only for a while? —(*Vār Asā*, 1)
Service:	Give up all calculations, Render service, as a servant humble. —(*Rāmkali*, 3)

From a spiritualistic viewpoint, ethics of Gurbāni indicates the path with orientation of values, for the realization of an ideal life. This is a way to apprehend the truth; a way to wash off the filth of untruth; a style of life whereby to cultivate the 'land' of one's being for sowing in it the seed of spiritual joy. From a purely ethical point of view, the moral elements contained in Gurbāni—with its love of enlightenment, humanistic orientation, and support for virtues—form a concrete basis for the excellence of the individual and community life of man. The God oriented (*gurmukh*) ones who have cultivated their selves,[21] are capable of establishing a well-ordered, well-knit human community. Ethics is not only a key to the spiritual welfare of the individual, it is also a worthy way of life, saturated with the discipline of virtuous acts and the vision of universal human welfare.

21 Cf *Mājh, Suhi, Asā*, 3.

7

The Sikh Society

The Śikh community holds its scripture, the holy Guru Granth (also called the Adi-Granth), as its spiritual mentor equivalent to the Guru in person. Primarily and fundamentally, the message of Guru Granth is spiritual, and only secondarily is it social and secular. In its primary function of an emancipator of the human soul, Gurbāni presents a poetic transcription of the beatific vision of the supreme reality that the thirty-six authors of the Granth had individually intuited. But however lofty the vision and however high the object of such vision, if the spiritual content of the poetic compositions does contain a message, the message is unmistakably addressed to mankind. Spiritualism has value, not for God, but for man. The problem of God itself is man's problem. The human individual who, for sustenance and support, look up to his companions and to the social order, sometimes looks beyond—for that ultimate support which he considers divine and transcendent. He expects God's grace to descend upon him. He desires the Almighty to serve him, to render assistance in the realizing of his goals, to give him succour and solace, health and security. Religion keeps on reminding him that the Divine is primary and human being, secondary. But is he convinced?

No doubt, Sikhism is a religious faith with its firm spiritualistic base, its puritan moral code and injunctions for the conduct of life—all geared to the attainment of the highest intuitional experience believed to transfigure the individual. All the same, Sikhism has a secular and institutional aspect, with a tradition of five centuries of social protest. I do not say that the Sikh faith offers a protest ideology of its own, on the pattern of socialism, radicalism or even nationalism. In spite of the elements of protest evident in the make-up of this faith, it can hardly be asserted that Sikhism, structured on the foundations of Gurbāni, is a socio-political doctrine thriving on a rigid formula of social protest. If the Sikh movement has been protestant in spirit and outlook, it was on account of the socio-secular and not the spiritual dimension of the faith. "Indeed," says Dr Niharranjan Ray, "the protestantism of the Sikhs was more total and all-pervasive. This community, because of its socio-temporal and activist attitude, grew up to be more and more socially and politically conscious, than the other protestant communities."[1]

A good number of scholars and interpreters of Sikhism are agreed that it has been a protestant movement from the beginning. Some compare it with the protestant Reformation of the sixteenth-century Europe. In the West, the advent of modern science, and more particularly the Copernican revolution, brought about a decisive break with the medieval thinking. The parallel revolutionary break with the mentality of passivity, as also with the conventional way of life, occurred in our land under the impact of Guru Nanak's personality, during the early sixteenth century. Historians may differ as to whether the founder of Sikhism was a reformer or a revolutionary. Some might insist, as did Indubhushan Banerjee, that Guru Nanak protested against conventionalism, and not against Hinduism; and that, in the hands of the Guru, Sikhism was not an altogether new creed.[2] This line of thinking views 'Sikhism as a Hindu movement aiming at the national regeneration of Hindus', or 'as an offshoot of traditional Hinduism and a response to the challenge of Islam'.

1 Niharranjan Ray (Ed.), *Sikhism and Indian Society*, Simla, 1967, p. 9.

2 Dr Fauja Singh (Ed), *Historians and Historiography of the Sikhs*, New Delhi, 1978, p. 260 (Dr J.S. Grewal's comments).

The Character of Sikh Movement

In the later history of the Punjab, there have been two movements of renaissance. The first, when Guru Nanak awakened the Punjabis from their deep slumber of conventionalism, passivity and fatalism, coupled with a rigid formalism and caste stratification. The second came more recently, when the Singh Sabha provided a momentum to the spread of enlightenment among the Sikh community of the Punjab. It is in regard to the first movement of renaissance that the opinions diverge. The theory that views the rise of Sikhism 'favourably', styling it as an 'institutionalized expression of Hindu nationalism', attempts to show the Sikhs as the vanguard of the Hindus, and Sikhism as the embodiment of Hindu reaction against Islam. While expounding this thesis, Gokal Chand Narang gives credit to the founder of Sikhism by saying that "Nanak left the Hindus of the Punjab immensely better than he had found them."[3] Niharranjan Ray puts a more liberal construction on the theory that the Sikh faith arose to "meet the challenge of the growing Islamic ideology in India." To begin with, Sikhism was "just a way of life, simple, pure, transparent, divested of all dross rituals, totems and taboos, fetishes and sham distinctions of caste." This was certainly a "negation of Hinduism at the popular level," though the commitment to absolute devotion to one and only one reality "was also an acceptance of the metaphysical interpretation of the *Brahman* at a higher level."[4]

Another line of argument traces the impact of Islam on Sikhism, but does not claim the latter to be an offshoot of Islam. It draws attention to several points of contact; for instance, the monotheistic faith, non-practice of idolatry and ritualism, similarity of the *jehād* and *dharam judh*, and the congregational mode of prayer. At best, the supporters of this theory, notably Arnold Toynbee, characterize Sikhism as a synthesis of Hinduism and Islam. Khushwant Singh puts the case of hybridization in the metaphor : "Sikhism was born out of wedlock between

3 Ibid , pp. 267-85 (Dr Fauja Singh's comments).
4 N. Ray, op. cit , p. 7.

Hinduism and Islam."[5] Mcleod's discussion of the subject also gives a like impression, but he is careful enough to 'state categorically' that he does not deny the originality of Guru Nanak's thought.[6] At any rate, the argument in favour of the synthesis theory has been best examined by Dr Paul B. Courtright, who, as he says, is "trying to dispel the simplistic notion that Sikhism is a conscious syncretism or that it is primarily an attempt to reconcile Hinduism and Islam." He believes that the formation of Sikhism "was a protest against pride of worship, scripture and caste." It was "a protest against conventionalism, and not against Hinduism and Islam as such."[7]

Dr Courtright's case deserves a fuller presentation. He sets out to examine the validity of categorizing Sikhism in the way of syncretism, against the picture of the Punjab torn by "confusion, the breakdown of social and political order, the conflict of armies, religious fanaticism, and ethnic transition" in Guru Nanak's period. Hinduism was retreating into orthodoxy and becoming more insistent upon ritual and the authority of the scriptures. Guru Nanak adopted the reformist response to the perversion and chaos of the times. It was out of the milieu of inter-religious contact of Bhakti and Sufism that Sikhism was born. "The main thrust of Guru Nanak's message was not theological and credal." His famous saying 'There is no Hindu, there is no Musalmān', "simply means that the communal identities are secondary to the worship of the true God."

Courtright further asserts : "Guru Nanak rejected the authority of both the Hindu and Muslim scriptures." If his chief purpose had been the reconciliation of the two traditions, he probably would have selected passages from the sacred literature of both Hinduism and Islam. Instead, Sikhism developed its own 'scriptural tradition' with Guru Nanak's writings at its centre. If at all there are affinities with Sufism in Guru Nanak's thought, these are the results of process of interpenetration which had already been going on before his time in the Bhakti

5 *A History of the Sikhs*, vol. I, p. 17.

6 Cf. Dr N. Ray, op. cit., p. 308.

7 Paul B. Courtright, *Essays in Honour of Dr Ganda Singh*, ed. Harbans Singh & N. Gerald Barrier, Patiala, 1976, p. 424.

tradition and Sufism. "Guru Nanak himself is not the syncretizing element in the development of Sikhism." Subsequently, Sikhism developed institutions of its own. These "developments show Sikhism's originality and uniqueness." The institution of "the guruship secured religious authority for the Sikhs outside Hindu and Islamic sources of authority." The use of vernacular in the writings of the *Adi-Granth* "brought a separate identity to Sikhism and helped establish a new literary tradition outside Sanskrit."

Disagreeing with Khushwant Singh's 'intriguing' argument of an infant Punjabi nationalism, Courtright explains the formation of the Khalsa in terms of a new brotherhood of believers. In a defensive response to Muslim persecution, Sikhism sought its own identity as a religious and political community. "Its organizational structure is more secular than it is patterned after organizations of the Bhakti or Sufi cults." Courtright is of the opinion that, to do justice to the Sikh tradition, it is imperative to recognize "the unique circumstances in the development of its identity as a genuinely new and original religious expression." Guru Nanak need not be seen as a reconciler and a synthesizer. "He was a purifier of the popular religious expressions of both traditions." Formation of Sikhism was an "attempt at simplification of religious worship and the concentration on the Name of the one God." "Consequently, to classify Sikhism as a syncretic religion will be a distortion."[8]

So much for the character of the Sikh movement. Needless to say that the foregoing assessment of the movement is broadly acceptable to the Sikh intellectual whose emotional make-up is tempered, as a matter of course, by affinities with Sikh culture.

Foundations of Sikh Institutions

What is the true nature of Sikhism which, apart from its ethico-spiritual dimension, is admitted to be a 'social' movement? We have to look for the answer in several directions, meeting some of the difficulties involved in the process. "The major impediment in understanding the true nature of Sikhism so far has

8 Ibid., pp. 418-31.

been the desire to explain it as a historical phase of the Hindu religious thought of medieval India."[9]—This is the opinion of Sirdar Kapur Singh. He proceeds to examine the nature of Hindu culture itself and locates its roots, firstly, in the hymns of Rig Veda with its recognition of social hierarchy, caste system and exclusive stress on ceremony and formal conformity of conduct. The other root is found in the reflections of the Upanishads, which recognize human equality in the spiritual sphere, and insist on the necessity of the inner culture and *sādhanā.* "The Hinduism which was shaken to its very foundations by the Muslim impact was in the five centuries preceding the rise of Guru Nanak, a body of customs and a body of ideas." The birth of Guru Nanak coincided with one of the most critical periods of the history of the Hindu race. "The organism of the Hindu society and Hindu culture had for the first time in its history, failed to absorb the shock of a foreign impact that of Islam, and to assimilate it." Guru Nanak set upon his "appointed task of laying down the foundations of a new society," insisting that a life lived in a social context and on an ethical plane is necessary for salvation. He placed his new society on a sound philosophic base. The content of salvation was not merely individual but collective and social. "These teachings of Guru Nanak entail fundamental and far-reaching social and political consequences, and the history of Punjab, henceforth inevitably, becomes the Sikh history."[10]

Sirdar Kapur Singh's assessment of the founder of the 'historical upsurge and movement known to history as Sikhism', reveals the Guru in a new perspective. For him, Guru Nanak is a most dynamic personality the world has ever seen. "Guru Nanak was neither a *bhakta*, in the historical sense of the word, nor an exponent of the Bhakti school of medieval India." His approach was one of 'transvaluation' of the existing faiths and cults; he ushered in a new spiritual era as well as a social and political era for the mankind. "As a divine, inspired thinker

9 Sirdar Kapur Singh, Guru Nanak Commemorative Lectures—1975, in 'Nanak Prakash Patrika', Patiala, June 1977, p. 9.
10 Ibid., pp. 2C-32.

and a religious teacher, Guru occupies a uniquely significant place in history."[11]

Most of the practices and institutions of the Sikhs are founded upon the teachings of Guru Nanak and his spiritual successors. The phychological discipline of *Sādhanā* is the purely religious aspect of the scheme, distinct from morality and ritual. "Its primary interest is centred around the problem of the quality of living and the transformation and evolution of the human mind and experience." Another principle of fundamental importance for the Sikh way of life is '*kirat*'—related to the problem of creation and possession of wealth. Here Sirdar Kapur Singh compares Guru Nanak's injunction with the Marxian theory of economic value. All material possessions acquired through dishonest means and exploitation of labour are not only sinful, but morally illegitimate and unjustified. The tenet of 'sharing' one's belongings with others, deals with the problems of the distribution of wealth and organization of power. Earnings of an honest, creative labour are to be socially owned, since "no individual is spiritually complete unless he considers himself as a part of the society as a whole,"—that is, the community or *Sangat*, which is placed one step higher than the Guru himself.[12] This last injunction brings to fore the problem of social organization.

Mankind has experimented with several forms of social organization and philosophers have toyed with still greater number of theories, both utopian and practicable. The question is not 'why' ought one obey the social authority at all ? For, "men do not choose to live in society, they are born into a society and into one of a particular structure. In rare instances they are in a position to exchange one form of society for another." "If there is to be a society, there must be some form of social organization : some set of institutions, some recognized machinery for taking decisions which will count as the decisions of the group as a whole. The machinery need not be democratic, but it must exist. This is a logical necessity;...The only question which arises is what form of social organization

11 Ibid., pp. 6-33.
12 Ibid., pp. 10-37.

to have."[13] Should the organization be based upon some sort of divine revelation and religious authority, or should it grow out of a secular basis? The Western protestant reformation did not support the Church in matters concerned with the organization of society. Philosophers like Hobbes and Locke, Kant and Hegel, Bentham and Marx offered a variety of theories, like social contract and kingdom of ends, utilitarianism and historical determinism, apart from the anarchists who refuse to recognize the obligation to obey any political authority.

The rise and growth of Sikhism has been seen as a 'reaction to the monolithic, rigid and close society' of the sixteenth century. "It corroded the fossilized social base of the political authority in the Punjab. Starting as a reform movement, it became an organised, well-knit, yet an open society during the Guru period."[14] Till the time of Guru Arjan, the Sikh movement continued as a peaceful religio-social movement; thereafter it acquired the colour of a political movement. A full, comprehensive and critical reconstruction of the development of Sikhism during the Guru period, has been attempted by Indubhushan Banerjee who finds 'several features of exceptional interest' in the movement. From the organizational point of view the most important step taken by Guru Nanak was the nomination of Angad as his successor. This succession marked the first cleavage between the Hindus and the Sikhs.[15] Gokal Chand Narang appears to suggest that the founder of Sikhism approached the problem from the national point of view, though by the nature of things he had to restrict the immediate scope of his work to the spiritual and moral education of his people. Guru Arjan gave the Sikhs their scripture, which "served as a code of sacred as well as secular Law."[16]

Ultimately, the foundations not only of the Sikh institutions, but also of the overall economic progress made by the Punjabi community, as also of the relative freedom from meaningless

13 A.J. Ayer, Philosophy and Politics, in *Metaphysics and Common Sense*, 1973.

14 *Historiography*, op cit., p. 212 (Reference is to Muhammed Latif by Dr S.K. Bajaj).

15 Ibid., pp. 243-8 (comments by A.C. Banerjee).

16 Ibid., pp. 269-71 (Dr Fauja Singh's comments),

taboos in the Punjab, are to be traced in the outlook and attitudes of poet-philosophers of Guru Granth, in regard to matters of the spirit, society and state. The problem, in the end, revolves round the personality of the Gurus and Bhaktas who composed the inspired poetry of the Granth. The person of Guru Nanak, for instance, is not the ordinary, egocentric individual, in the sense of a natural biological category. The differentiation of his 'person' may perhaps be described best in terms employed by Nikolai Berdyaev. "The personality is a spiritual category," he says. "The personality is the direct expression of the impact of the spirit on man's physical and psychical nature." "The personality is above all an axiological category : it is the manifestation of an existential purpose." "It is sensitive to all of the currents of social and cosmic life and open to a variety of experience, but it takes care not to lose its identity in society or in the cosmos." Personality supposes creative action and the 'conquest of self'. It is capable of both joy and suffering. The true personality is attained only through conflict and an ascension into the realm of spirit. "Man is everlastingly solitary beneath his disguise." But, from a metaphysical standpoint, "the personality is social because it feels the need of communicating with others." Personality concentrates in itself the whole 'mystery of Being, of creation'.[17] The characteristics of personality, revealed by Berdyaev's philosophic insight, belong in full measure to Guru Nanak and the rest of the authors of Guru Granth.

The Protestant Spirit of Gurbani

Gurbāni may broadly be viewed as a critique of life. It touches all aspects of human life, solitary and individual, moral and social, sectarian and humanistic. It portrays man in the roles of householder, of thinker, of devotee; he may be a preacher and pedant, ruler and leader, Gurmukh and Brahman-gyāni. Gurbāni depicts man in a variety of social contexts and situations; its range is as wide as the whole span of human life, from

17 N. Berdyaev, *Solitude in Society*. (Selection reprinted in *A Modern Introduction to Metaphysics*, ed. D.A. Drennen, 1968.)

infancy to death, from ego-centricity to God-realization. Man's follies and sins, his customs and policies, his predicament and alienation—nothing escapes the synoptic vision of the seers and sages of the *Adi-Granth.* In the course of all this description of human affairs, they have produced and bequeathed to us a literary treasure full of high social relevance. If ethico-spiritual is one major theme of the thought-content of Gurbāni, socio-cultural is the other. Both share a common objective, namely, welfare of man.

Is the man of religion essentially a social creature, according to Gurbāni ? In what consists the religious quest ? One answer is that religion in its 'purest sense' is separated from its social and ethical content. "It is the *adhyātam vidyā* of the Upanishadic sages," says Kapur Singh. He recalls A. N. Whitehead's expression in regard to what he calls the loftiest conception of religion in the West.[18] In fact, "Whitehead's famous characterization of religion as 'what the individual does with his own solitariness' has been much quoted and much misunderstood." Professor John E. Smith's interpretation of the saying makes an important point. "Whitehead tells us that the statement was intended to deny the claim that religion is primarily a *social* fact. It is not that religion is unrelated to the social character of every reality, but rather that religion has to do with the person considered *in himself.* The formula expresses more than the vague sense that religion demands quiet and solitude." He adds : "Every person takes on a universal character in the sense that having a worth in himself, he does not derive it from being a member of some special group."[19]

Hartshorne who has applied some of the key-concepts in Whitehead's philosophy to theological studies, sharply criticizes those who rejoice in the aloofness of God. "The true God is instead the eternal sympathizer who is concerned for man and the struggle in which he is engaged." Hartshorne's argument proceeds on these lines : "If God is unqualifiedly absolute and complete in himself, then it is difficult to understand how he can

18 Sirdar Kapur Singh, op. cit., p. 11.

19 John E. Smith, in *Religion* (Princeton Studies) ed. Paul Ramsey et. al., 1965.

love and how he can care. As perfect in the simple sense, God can be immutable substance but not person." Then follows his bold stroke : "being perfect in the sense of excluding the imperfect," is "inferior to a perfection that includes both. In being internally related to the world, including man and his tragedy and evil along with his progress in self-realization, God surpasses himself in the sense of abstract, eternal, non-relative perfection." Love, says Hartshorne, defined as social awareness, taken literally, is God.[20]

I have referred to the "solitary" character of the religious man and to the "social" nature of God, in two of the influential modern thinkers, in order to bring home the intent of Gurbāni on the themes of a loving and gracious super Being, and the essentially non-attached man of the world completely in tune with the absolute Person. The God of spiritual devotees and the Gurus is the benevolent, indulgent God, conceived on the pattern of man, sharing with him emotions that are human. The *bhaktas* would not communicate with an incommunicable Deity, rapt in Himself, indifferent to the lot of His people, pleading ignorance of what goes on in the world below. They pray to Him, firmly convinced that He would listen; they offer Him their loving devotion in good faith, and are prepared to act according to his bidding.

The poet-philosophers of Guru Granth are essentially nonconformists; they adhere to free thinking and express their thoughts and sentiments without let or hindrance. One who is obliged to act in conformity with the established custom, sectarian practice or political authority, under any type of coercion, accepts for himself a role in which he cannot act conscientiously. He is forced to lead an inauthentic life, with little scope for raising the voice of protest. However, the spirit of protest in the case of a poet-philosopher or *bhakta* takes on a form quite distinct from the forms it assumes in statesmen, political leaders and revolutionaries. The social protest in Gurbāni is singularly free from the spirit of violence, or ill-will against any kind of authority, or bad faith in general. In some cases,

20 Ibid., pp. 444-5.

the tone is mild and gentle, but in a few instances the protest is quite loud, vociferous and altogether convincing.

The Gurus and Bhaktas are not simply poet-philosophers; they are profoundly religious and moral in their make-up. They legislate not only for themselves, but also for their fellow-men, indeed for humanity. The poet of Guru Granth is not merely an individual, he is properly a 'person', assimilating in his personality something of the supra-personal. He is in a position to speak for others and to others, with a unique sense of responsibility. To qualify for this role, he acquires that 'fullness of life' which integrates all his faculities. "In religious reality the person has concentrated himself into a whole, for it is only as a unified being that he is able to live religiously."[21] This observation of Martin Buber is fortified by Father Lotz, for whom philosophy is characterized by a loving knowledge, and religion by a knowing love. He believes: "The full response of man to the challenge of being is neither the knowing-insight of metaphysics nor the loving submission of religion. It is in both. Each in its own way is the bearer of totality. Mataphysics is pointed to religion to keep the submission of love alive, while religion is pointed to metaphysics to provide the necessary insight."[22]

The man of religion, with the poetic sensibility and philosophic vision of the order of Gurbāni, would address himself to the problems of man and society from a perspective marked with balance and profundity. In their poetic compositions, the authors of Guru Granth have occasionally turned attention to the social challenges of their times and tackled them in a protestant spirit. In their criticism of life and its flaws, they speak the discontent of their age. In their poetic protest, they voice the feelings and urges of the lowly and down-trodden, the exploited and oppressed sections, indeed the suffering humanity.

The whole social outlook of the Sikhs is shaped by the values and virtues enucinated in the *Adi-Granth*, even though the customs and rituals have come to be established under the

21 Martin Buber, in Drennen (Ed.), op. cit.
22 Johannes Lotz, in Drennen (Ed.), op. cit.

impact of tradition that is older than the advent of Sikh ideology. Certain local factors too have influenced the forms of cultural observances of the community in the different regions of the Punjab and elsewhere. But the greatest single factor common to all the various ritualistic patterns and beliefs, is the allegiance to the teaching enshrined in the Granth, in regard to the emanation of all values of life from the one supreme Creator-Person, and in regard to the melioristic orientation of the Sikh view of life with its motto of *Sarbatt dā Bhalā* (i.e., welfare of all mankind).

8

The Theme of Protest in Gurbani

Gurbāni is no philosophy of protest.

The modern society has witnessed several forms of agitation and protest, ranging from strikes and fasts to rebellion and mutiny. Gandhiji developed the technique of non-violent protest known to us as Satyagrah. The philosopher Bertrand Russell has described in his *Autobiography* the mass civil disobedience, practised by his fellow-citizens under his enlightened supervision. Whereas the Bhaktas and Gurus are known to have participated in the people's struggles and put up physical resistance to oppression of all kinds, their poetry does not outline any doctrinaire approach to the methodology of protest, comparable to the techniques and ideologies of social protest evolved in our day. The spirit of protest in Gurbāni expresses itself in forms compatible with the aesthetic sensibility of the spirit-born poets of the *Adi-Granth.* Kabir and Guru Nanak are the key-figures representative of the Bhaktas and the Gurus, whose expressions set the tone of protest in Gurbāni, which, in this context, includes Bhakta-Bāni as well.

Protest against Human Folly

The compositions of Guru Nanak and his spiritual colleagues contain numerous references to their sense of protest against the imbalance as also the lack of justice and propriety in human affairs. Each one of them, in his own poetic way, expresses the spirit of protest in a phrase or a couplet, and sometimes in a total hymn. The defining mark of social protest may be seen in Guru Nanak's enunciation :

> If the mighty molest the mighty
> No feeling of protest rises in my mind ;
> But, should a ferocious tiger attack the feeble herd
> I would question even my Lord.
>
> (Guru Nanak; p. 360)

The sense of protest in Kabir takes on a delightful form. In one instance, when soliciting attention to the privations suffered by him as a devotee, he confronts the Divine with the ultimatum :

> I can't keep on meditating on a hungry stomach
> Here, have Thy rosary back, My Lord !
>
> (Kabir; p. 656)

In either of the instances quoted, God has been made a party to the situation obtaining in life. This perhaps is a constant reminder of the mode of protest in Gurbāni, which of course makes a multitude of objects and situations its target of complaint. If a random sample of illustrative couplets is taken, the expressions of protest may conveniently fall into three main categories : first, against several forms of human folly; second, against the established social and political authority of an oppressive nature; third, against the seeming indifference to the human predicament on the part of the Almighty. The folly that evokes poetic protest, is not confined to ritualism, idolatry and vices of egoism, but covers intemperance, blind faith and, above all, ignorance which is never rated as bliss in Gurbāni. "The disciples, whose preceptor is ignorant, shall commit follies too"—says Guru Amar Dās—(p. 951). Kabir offers the comment : "what can the holy Satguru do, if the deficiency lies with the disciples, who in their ignorance do not reform themselves?" —(p. 1372).

There is no end to the count of ignorant fools in the world, for whom Guru Nanak almost shows impatience. In Japuji, he refers to the "innumerable people at the receiving end who acknowledge not the divine gifts; innumerable are the fools who keep on eating and consuming for life."—(Stanza 25). "Countless are the fools, utterly stupid and senseless; countless are the tbieves partaking the stolen wealth."—(Stanza 18). He chides those engrossed merely in the worldly pursuits :

Cursed is the life that is led
Only to eat and swell the belly.

(Guru Nanak; p. 790)

It is necessary to acquire some knowledge and learning, says Kabir, in order to discipline the mind.—(p. 340). But it is no use simply repeating 'knowledge, knowledge' as every one seems to do. This generates pride and suffering; yet no one desists from it.—(Guru Nanak; p. 831). "Spiritually blind and covered with the filth of ignorance, however much he may try to cleanse himself, his soul is no whit purified ; without Divine truth all ritual is a husk deluding man like the juggler's tricks." —(Guru Nanak ; p. 1343)[1] "How can the lamp be lit without the oil ?"—protests Guru Nanak (p. 25). And "those who pride themselves without cultivating any virtue, are really the asses."—(Guru Nanak ; p. 1246).

There are several expressions of human ignorance which become the objects of criticism and protest in Gurbāni; for instance, the custom of *satti* and initiation ceremonies ; superstitions like *sūtak* and ritualistic purification of the kitchen; indifference to the 'secrets of alphabet'—not to talk of *nād* and *Veda* or aesthetic discrimination. Another expression of ignorance is fear and cowardice which ought to yield place to positive courage and forbearance. Guru Tegh Bahadur's dictum—

Not to frighten anyone : Nor to be afraid !—(p. 1427)

serves not only as a mark of valiance and bravery, but also of wisdom and foresight.

1 Trans. Prof. G.S. Talib.

Out of his ignorance, man indulges in idolatry. Kabir protests to the gardener plucking flowers and leaves—that each of the petals is endowed with life. "The stone-idol, to worship whom the petals are gathered, is a mere lifeless stone."—(p. 479). Ravidās in a similar vein tries to bring home the fact that "the milk we offer to the temple-idol, has been polluted by the calf ; the flower is defiled by the flying insect; the water is contaminated by the fish."—(p. 525). Namdev is in complete agreement with Ravidās; he forbids us to defile the gods with impure, polluted water, containing 'forty two lakhs of germs'—(p. 485). He further argues—"We bow our head before one piece of stone, that is idol, but just trample over another stone. If the one is god, is not the other one god as well ?"—(p. 525). The pilgrims who fondly believe that by visiting the holy banks and taking bath in the sacred pools, all their sins would be washed away, receive a concentrated rebuke :

> A good man is good even without wash
> A thief is but a thief, howsoever soaked.
>
> (Guru Nanak; p. 789).

In his negligence, man ignores the fact of his alienation from the primordial essence and spiritual origin. Guru Amar Dās exhorts him: "Know your essence, man; you embody the very light of the Lord."—(p. 441). Kabir's dictum that all human beings be treated equally, is of the same piece. Allah is the sole primary source of all—(p. 1349). And if the Lord resides within, it is a folly to look for him without—(Guru Nanak; p. 722). Farid too warns against wasting one's time searching for the Divine in the forest. "Find him inside your heart, man; what will you gain by roaming about in wilderness, except for trampling the thorns under your feet ?"—(p. 1378).

The onslaught against the folly of caste-pride is quite vehement in both Kabir and Guru Nanak; by contrast, Ravidās and Namdev register only a mild protest. The force of Kabir's dialectic seems to be at its height when he confronts the *brahmin* :

If you are a brahmin born of Brahmā,
Why were you not born differently ?
How can you claim to be Brahmā-born ?
And how am I a low-caste ?
If it is blood that runs in my veins,
Is it milk running in yours ?

—(p. 324)

Guru Nanak cautions man : "Let no one feel proud about his caste. Is the *brahmin* really born of Brahmā ? Don't entertain pride of caste, O simpleton fool ; lest a host of evils should flow from it."—(p. 1128). Ravidās is content to articulate his feelings about his caste, his lineage and his birth—all being 'inferior'—(p. 486). He has no hesitation in calling himself 'Ravidās Chamār'. But, his God is great : "Whose 'contagion' pollutes the people, Thou lift them up to Thyself. My protector Lord who fears none, raises the lowly to heights."—(p. 1106). And Namdev is satisfied confiding in his God—"These *pandits* treat me with contempt; I seek Thy shelter, O Lord."—(p. 1292). He wonders why he was born in the family of calico-printers,—not permitted to enter the shrine—(p. 1164). The excellent summing-up, however, is found in Guru Nanak's couplet :

Caste is hollow, fame is hollow
The one Saviour protects all fellows. —(p. 83)

Protest against Unjust Establishment

That Guru Nanak was sensitive to the political upheavals of his times, is amply evidenced in the hymns popularly known as Bābarvāni is the Asā and Tilang *rāgas*. In the *Vār Mājh* and *Vār Asā*, several stanzas speak of the devastation, torture and plunder at the hands of aggressors, and refer to the corrupt practices of the ruling cliques. The vulnerable subjects—helpless victims of oppression—indulging in hypocrisy and bad faith to save their skin, are also depicted. To give a few illustrations:

Babar has descended upon India with the wedding-party
of lust and forcibly demands surrender of the bride.
Decency and law have hidden themselves;
the evil is strutting about in triumph.
Mohammadan and Hindu priests are discarded,
and Satan is solemnising the marriages.

(Guru Nanak; p. 722)[2]

You impose taxes on the cow and the Brahmin;
And yet will cow-dung which you worship get you emancipation?
You wear dhotis, put paste-marks on your
forheads and handle beads;
Yet you live on earnings made from Muslims
whom you call Mlechhas (evil-minded);
Secretly you practise Hindu worship-rituals,
but make a show of reading Muslim books,
and observe the Turks' (Muslims') customs;
Discard hypocrisy !

(Guru Nanak; p. 471)[3]

The Gurus protested against the ways of the people in contemporary age, the so-called Kaliyuga:

The beggar adopts the title Patshah (king)
and the fool calls himself Pundit.
The blind is named discriminating judge;
—this way they waste their lives.
The evil-doer is called the leader (chowdhury);
—everywhere prevails the untruth.

(Guru Angad; p. 1288)

The law of Kaliyuga is such that one who practises truthfulness, comes to grief—(GN, p. 902). "The age is turned knife; rulers butchers; righteousness hath flown away on wings. The dark night of evil is spread; the moon of righteousness is visible

2 Trans. G.S. Talib.
3 Trans. G.S. Talib.

nowhere : I have groped and groped to madness,—in this thick darkness, no path is visible. The whole world wails in suffering, gripped in egoism"—(Guru Nanak; p. 145)[4]

The kings are tigers, the headmen are dogs—
They go and awaken those sleeping in peace.
(Guru Nanak; p. 1288)[5]

Apart from the cruel political set-up, some organized sections of society, the self-appointed teachers of the people, the so-called *siddhas* and *yogis* and the temple administrators—all come handy for criticism for their conduct. A line symbolic of Guru Nanak's protest against all these forces, reads:

Disgraceful is the life of those
who sell the name of God.
—(p. 1245)

Kabir gives a graphic desciption of the pious-looking *sādhus* "wearing three and a half yards long *dhotis* and three-fold *janeoo* cords; adorning rosaries around their necks and carrying bright bowls in hands; let them not be mistaken for the devotees of God; they are really the cheats of Benāras (*Banaras ke Thug*)"—(Kabir; p. 476). He castigates the professional *brahmin* class that perpetuates senseless rituals among the public. His sarcasm is sharp and blunt, as for instance in regard to the custom of *sarādh*:

No one reveres the elders during their lifetime
But people observe *sarādhs* when the elders pass away.
The poor dead ones are not recipients of food,
The crows and dogs consume it instead.
—(Kabir; p. 332)

Namdev rejects the claims to divine knowledge publicized by preachers.—"Hindu is blind and Muslim purblind. Gyāni is

4 Trans. G S. Talib.
5 Trans. Bhai Jodh Singh.

wiser than the two. Hindu worships the temple, Musalmān the mosque. Namdev prays the Lord unbounded by *mandir* or *masjid*."—(p. 875). It all depends upon the search one makes; for "the supreme essence pervading the universe, is the same as is present in the frame of the body."—(Pipā; p. 695). "One need not tear off the common dress and take to the blanket of the recluse. The Master is to be found within one's home, if only the intention is clear."—(Guru Amar Dās; p. 1383).

Gurbāni offers a critique of the ideology and practice of the *yogi* and *siddha* sects. The Gurus did not commend the matted locks of the yogis and the dust and ash they smear their bodies with. Instead of the physical feats and the paraphernalia of the recluses, the Gurus prescribed a mental and moral discipline to be adopted by the householder. In Gurbāni, there is no dearth of instances that support the family-life, in preference to the life of a *yogi* or *avadhūta* who, for his food, has to turn to the very people whose way of life he forsakes in contempt. The recluse puts up the show of abjuring food and vainly throws away pleasures. "In the pursuit of delusions he undergoes much suffering; unclad day and night he tortures his body; under a vow of silence he strays from the true path;...the blind fool, in the end he only repents."—(Guru Nanak; p. 467).[6] According to Gurbāni, "yoga lies not in the begging-pouch, in carrying a staff; nor in smearing over with ashes;... Yoga consists not in sitting in cremation spots, nor in falling into trances; nor lies it in wandering about the world, nor in ritual bathing. To live immaculate amidst the impurities of the world—that is the true yoga-practice."—Guru Nanak; p. 730)[7]

Protest against Divine Indifference

The devotee, more than the philosopher, has an abiding faith in the righteousness of God. He is not easily deterred by the empirical presence of evil in the world. Nevertheless, even this deep seated faith is over-shadowed occasionally by the anguish to which man is often subjected. The devotee, if he happens to

6 Trans. G.S. Talib.
7 Trans. G.S. Talib.

be a poet, gives expression to his feelings of perturbance through his aesthetic medium. The supreme example of the poetic protest of this kind, is the well-known couplet in Guru Nanak's Bābarvāni :

> People suffered endless tortures, and wailed,
> Didst Thou have no compassion for them ?
>
> —(p. 360)

The implication seems to be that the Almighty Creator of the world, had He so willed, could have prevented the untold misery of His creatures. But, the still deeper implication, perhaps, is the underlying faith that even this evil was necessary; perhaps there is a Divine purpose involved which we mortals fail to visualize and appreciate.

If the world is burning in the fire of folly, if suffering is man's inevitable fate, if there be no escape from evils,—whose indifference is responsible for all this ? Guru Amar Dās directs his appeal for mercy to the Divine and to none else :

> Save this burning world through Thy grace, O Lord !
> Lift us to whichever door of salvation Thou decidest.
>
> —(p. 853)

In a delightful composition in Rāmkali *rāga*, Guru Arjan tellingly addresses the Omnipotent :

> (Thou art really a hard nut to crack!)
>
> Whatever effort may we make, Thou art not pleased.
> Thou art not won over, whatever scriptures may we read.
> Thou art not controlled through ablutions at holy spots,
> Thou art not conquered through conquest of the globe.
> Not through intellectual feats art Thou caressed,
> Nor through bountiful charities art Thou impressed.
> Thou controlest all, O infinite transcendent Lord,
> Thy devotees alone control Thee—with power
> that Thou affordst.
>
> —(p. 962)

Guru Arjan refuses to contemplate the Master in the usual formations, as either Allah or Rām,—He is above the distinctions carved out by the believers. "I do not set out for the Haj, nor for the Tirthas." "I perform not *pooja*, nor say the *namāz* " "I am no Hindu and no Musalmān."—(p. 1136). Kabir, to whom this hymn of Guru Arjan is addressed, fully shares these sentiments. He expressly asserts—"There is no dispute about me : I have given up both the Pandit and the Mullah."—(p. 1158)

Ravidās's protest against the divine indifference is transmuted into rationalization :

O my infinite Lord,
If we humans did not commit sins
How wouldst Thou be known as Forgiver ?

—(p. 93)

And Farid's eloquent protest takes the form of "either : or"—reminding us of the slogan—"Give me liberty or give me death."

Says he :

O Farid, may I never lose my liberty
Be this the Lord's will;
If I deserve not my independence
Let Him put my life to end.

—(p. 1380)

Two of the Bhaktas, Kabir and Dhanna, composed two hymns remarkably similar in spirit and orientation—as if laying down 'conditions' for their *bhakti.* They beseech the Divine to provide for not only two square meals daily, but also a bed and bedding complete with the pillow and quilt, plus a milch cow, and a horse to ride, in addition, of course, to a fine-tempered wife.—(Kabir, p. 656; Dhanna, p. 695). Kabir goes a step further. He explains that in asking for the bread and butter ration, he has not been greedy; he assures God that, in fulfilment, he would absolutely devote himself to His *bhakti.*— "Saith Kabir, let the mind be appeased; With the fulfilment of the mind, comes cognition of the Divine."

—(p. 656)

Note.—All page references in the text are to Guru Granth.

9

Value-System of Guru Gobind Singh

The short span of Guru Gobind Singh's life was a constant challenge to the Moghul empire entrenched in India. He departed from the general line of passive protests and pacifism adopted by generations of native communities and his own predecessors, in relation to the State policy. A parallel to the Guru's armed action is available in his contemporary Shivaji's performance, who threw the gauntlet to Aurangzeb's military might. In our own day, Subhash Chander Bose challenged the British empire with the handful of trained and disciplined sons of the soil, simultaneously with the experiment of passive resistance that was conducted on a massive scale. In each case, it was the concrete situation and the circumstances which prompted the leaders of men to take to the sword.

It may be surmised that the martyrdom of his father, Guru Tegh Bahadur, under orders of Aurangzeb, led Guru Gobind Singh to rise in revolt against the Moghul power. He might have felt within him an impulsion to crush the headstrong ruling hierarchy. But it may not exactly have been a feeling of vengeance. It was righteous indignation at the cowardly and dastardly execution of his father. It is interesting to note that Guru Gobind Singh's grandfather had also organized an armed band following the tortures leading to death of his father, Guru Arjan Dev, during Jehangir's regime. The precedent may have provided a cue and added strength to the Guru, who had definitely imbibed the anti-feudal spirit of Guru Nanak and his successors. It was thus not a question of personal feelings alone; motivation for military preparedness and armed operations must have come from the totality of conditions coupled with foresight. The Guru decided to make 'hawks' out of 'doves', by inspiring them with a fresh mode of thinking and acting.

The Almighty Deity

A unique stroke of the Guru's creative genius was his invoking of the stubborn aspect of the supreme Spirit. He called it by the epithet of 'all-steel' and 'double-edged sword'. It is significant that in a country with centuries of spiritualist tradition behind, Guru Gobind Singh saw fit to infuse the new animation into his companions through the familiar language of theology and mythology. In terms of his own philosophy, the Absolute Spirit is formless and featureless, colourless and casteless. Not a quality can we attribute to it; 'Neti, Neti' is the cry defying all description of it. This side of the picture refers to the Essence, i.e. the formless Being. The other side is the physical universe, or creation. It is the nagation of Neti, and is an affirmation of the expressiveness of the Absolute Spirit. He also characterizes the Spirit as *Kaal* (Time) in the temporal sense, and *Akaal* (Eternity) in the transcendent sense.[1]

Guru Nanak and his successors had resolved the opposition between the formless 'essence' and physical 'existence' by the formula of essence-in-existence, which they termed *Nām*. The Brahman and the phenomenal world dissolve in the synthesis of the space-time world throbbing with spirit. Guru Gobind Singh seems to have invested this *spirit* with creative values. He counts the attributes of Truth in terms of activities and acts in his composition 'Jaap'. The essential, creative principle operating in the universe is the reservoir of all values. Men

1 Dr S. Radhakrishnan says: "The absolute is the prius of all actuality and possibility. ...This universe is for the absolute only one possibility. Absolute is the pre-cosmic nature of God, and God is thé Absolute from the cosmic point of view."

have invoked different sets of values at different stages of the human history. Prophets have emphasized, in consonance with the need of their times, various aspects of the divine essence permeating the spatio-temporal framework. Guru Gobind Singh brought into focus the value of an inviolate force and presented it in terms of the 'wielder of the sword' and 'all steel'.

The ideal of the almighty deity had been postulated several times before the advent of Guru Gobind Singh, in order either to inspire men to be brave and mighty, or to instill the awe of God's majesty into their minds. The Guru held the ideal of powerful Master with a view to encouraging virtues of fortitude and valour in his followers. He bent all efforts in this direction. He prescribed a daily programme of drill and practice of the arms. He managed to secure all the necessary equipment for his soldier devotees, including the horses and a big drum, the *Ranjit Nagārā.* Development of the physique was the order of the day.

Such insistent emphasis on the physical culture might suggest as if the Guru were intent on producing a Spartan community in the hilly tracts of the Punjab. It is true that he desired to reshape the subjugated sections of population and prepare them for the struggles ahead. But he never chose the physical aspect of culture to the exclusion and at the expense of all other aspects. If he would be remembered for his cult of heroism, he would all the more be remembered for his cult of love. If he was a statesman and a patriot, he was also a poet of high order and spiritual mentor in direct succession to Guru Nanak. He did not preach mere 'meditation with closed eyes', in total oblivion of the world around. He proclaimed from the house-top:

> Listen all of you, I verily speak:
> Those alone realize the Lord
> Who tread the path of love.

Besides valour he placed the virtue of love. In the order of values, he made a significant addition—he showed the friendly, lovable aspect of the Spiritual Being. The aesthetic and poetic values of his times are abundantly present in his verse.

The Saint-Soldier

In the background of the Value-philosophy of Guru Gobind Singh had been the saintly heritage of Guru Nanak and Kabir. While he accepted the challenge posed by the ruling power and adopted the posture of strength, he attempted a devetailing of saintly and soldierly virutes amog his disciples. He seems to have foreseen the crumbling edifice of the Moghul rule, the weakening of the country's defences, and the possibility of fresh foreign invasions. He therefore decided to bring up a generation not only of freedom-fighters and protectors, but also of morally fortified individuals. The danger was obvious. His followers, when they got an upper hand, might fall a prey to corruption and moral degeneration. He was of course in great hurry; there was no time to lose. No broad-based, long-term plan could be effectively carried out; only an expedient had to be worked out rather quickly. The result was a re-cast ritual of baptism, vows of personal discipline, and certain forms of self-denial for those who joined the brotherhood of *Khālsā*. Whereas it is true that Guru Gobind Singh decried ostensible ritual and empty formalities in the performance of religious duties, he was justified in combining a measure of custom with reflection. The soldier-saints were to be moulded out of human material, which was on the whole native and simple, partly steeped in make-believe and superstition. The Guru, as we know, flourished three centuries before our times.

The circumstances warranted a moral code. Apart from carrying out the routine of physical culture, and the reading and reciting of the sacred word, the disciple was enjoined to cultivate purity and truthfulness in personal life, as well as social virtues and co-operation in the corporate life. For instance, it was nothing short of a radical departure from the prevailing feudal morality to insist on chastity and monogamy. Normal status of woman was never equal to the status of man in that pre-democratic age. It is a tribute to the fair-minded approach and democratic vision of Guru Gobind Singh to recognize in him the precursor of a new moral code based on mutual loyalty and love. Secondly, the institution of family and marriage was upheld. No self-denial or eradication of normal human emotions was preached. The teaching points to the cardianal virtue of Temperance, recommended in all matters of physical pleasure. Enumerating the qualities of a truly contemplative life, Guru Govind Singh counted three hedonistic disciplines: moderation in eating (*alap ahaar*), moderate sleep (*sulap nindrā*), and chastity in sex-life (*sheel*). Extending this principle to other motives, he counselled control over egoism, anger, infatuation and dogmatic tendencies.

Relevance of the virtues of chastity and integrity can be better appreciated in the present age, when the environment is full of temptations, distractions and opportunities for immodest living, to an extent that never was. These qualities of character derive from the over-all virtue of truthfulness, which is in turn an expression of Truth as one of the supreme values of human life. Gandhji's insistence on Truth as the highest value and its expression in the form of non-violence in human character, can be better appreciated in this light. In its broadest sense, non-violence is equal to truthfulness; it takes the form of purity in reflective life, honesty in mutual relations and justice in the social context. Cognitively, the pursuit of truth means acquisition of knowledge and the gathering of wisdom. Guru Nanak had used the symbol of Veda for wisdom, and called it an instrument for the bringing about of fulfilment in life. Guru Gobind Singh likewise accorded a high place to the instrument of wisdom contained in the scriptures. His efforts at having the Puranic, mythological literature translated, and the encouragement provided to the poets of his court are eloquent testimony to his faith in learning and wisdom.

Principles of Human Dignity

Let us turn to the values of social and corporate life. The trio of liberty, equality and fraternity has been popular enough in modern times since the French Revolution. But its Indian counterpart, viz. the values enunciated and promoted in practice by Guru Gobind Singh, is not so well known. Perhaps the followers of the Sikh faith did not realize the great academic significance of the institutions set up by the Guru. Moreover, India lagged behind Europe in the introduction of industrial relations and the accompanying democratic processes. Soon after the departure of Guru Gobind Singh from the scene, feudal forces and elements in the Sikh society gained dominance and control over weaker sections. Political instability, bitter animosity against the Sikh movement and the ensuing struggle for existence of the community during the eighteenth century, contributed to the neglect of these values. It will not be a travesty of the truth to say that the rule of Ranjit Singh over the Punjab and other north-western territories, was after all a rule of feudal power. Now that the democratic experiment has been conducted, and people have become alive to the values of democracy, the foresight and zeal of Guru Gobind Singh can be properly appreciated. Even if we do not dilate upon the economic and historical factors, we cannot deny the value of the following principles and institutions established by Guru Gobind Singh :

(1) *Work.*—They used to call it *Kirt*, that is, labour done by the hand. The Guru desired to raise work to the level of the prime want of life. He forbade parasitism of all types. Do honest labour and earn your livelihood—was the instruction. This is an indication of the sound moral base provided to the economic life of the Guru's disciples.

(2) *Welfare.*—Another commandment was to contribute ten per cent of one's earnings to the common fund, to be utilized for welfare activities. Schools, free kitchens for the pilgrims, and dwelling places (*serais*) were attached to the religious centres. Owing to lack of popular vigilance, such funds were of course misused and misappropriated occasionally. But, nobility of the motive behind the precept can hardly be questioned. Besides, all able-bodied individuals were enjoined to do some manual labour daily for the benefit of the community. This included cleaning of utensils, sweeping of the shrine premises, arranging for the comforts of pilgrims, and so on.

(2) *Equality before the Guru and the congregation.*—This was a healthy socializing practice. It accelerated liberation from the caste-shackles. None was inferior before the Guru; congregation was a brotherhood of equals. But this was not to be construed

as a step towards the classless organization of society. No conscious or systematic attempt was made to abolish economic differences or re-orient the vocational pursuits of the people. The precept applied to purely social and spiritual aspects of life.

(4) *Executive Council.*—A special democratic procedure established by Guru Gobind Singh was the nomination of an executive, consisting of the 'Five Chosen-ones', like the *sarpanch* in a *panchāyat*. All matters of vital importance to the community were to be referred to this council for deliberation and decision as to the course to be adopted. The entire congregation was expected to participate in the popular voice-vote on the proposals formulated by the executive, which were to be carried by *sarab-samiti* (unanimity) or *bahu-samiti* (majority decision). The congregation was the prototype of modern general assembly. Difficulties however were bound to arise in this case too. Power motive, lack of systematic training in the democratic procedures, and the concentration of funds in a few hands quite often led to denial of fair-play. Moreover, which *five* were the truly representative 'chosen ones' for the entire community ?

(5) *Humanism.*—The role of a prophet or religious teacher is not limited to a satisfactory interpretation of God's attributes and qualities; he must place *man* in the centre and use his good offices to bring him solace and salvation. Guru Gobind Singh was one of those spiritual leaders who acted not only on the religious plane, but on the social and political planes in order to ameliorate the lot of fellow humans. He addressed man *qua* man, without the narrow distinctions and antagonisms of the East and West, Hindu and Muslim, Masjid and Mandir. The West was not so prominent a factor of influence in India, during the seventeenth century. Nevertheless, the writings and teachings of the Guru resound with international, humanistic overtones:

> Temple and Mosque are not distinct;
> Puja and Nimaz mean the same.
> 'Homo sapiens' I recognize as one single race.

The action of Bhai Kanhaya, who supplied water to the injured soldiers, irrespective of their religious affiliations, won the whole-hearted approval of the Guru.

Fearlessness and Enlightenment

The eventful life-story of Guru Gobind Singh spotlights another significant value. It is equipoise: that blissful state of being which the Guru maintained in the most abnormal and trying circumstances. It is a tribute to his well-balanced, rational outlook on life to recognize that he did not commit the 'genetic fallacy' of condemning an entire community. "The division of whole populations into 'good' and 'bad' is a childish habit fostered by fairy tales," says Bertrand Russell. "We are all of us a mixture of good and bad, and there is not a preponderance of good on the side of those who are filled with self-righteousness." Of course we admire the Guru's bravery, his heroism, his gallantry. Yet he was primarily and fundamentally a man of peace. Resort to force was necessitated by the pressure of circumstances. The goddess Durga had been created in order that the monsters could be punished and exterminated. Almost in the midst of battles and war-cries, the Guru could carry on with the production and translation of literary works and the composing of sublime verse, with perfect equanimity The historic second edition of the *Adi-Granth* was compiled at Damdama Sahib while he was migrating from the Punjab to the South, virtually chased and surrounded by the hostile Moghul forces. His well-known Zafarnāmā in verse, addressed to Aurangzeb, was written while he was actually taking shelter in a village, hotly pursued by the enemy regiments.

Non-violence or pacifism was not a creed with Guru Gobind Singh, nor was voilence adopted for the fun of it. It was actually necessary and justified, since the violent violation of the traditional Indian way of life was impossible to stop by any other means. The execution of Guru Teg Bahadur had brought the matters to brink. His martyrdom was the last word in passive resistance. Guru Tegh Bahadur attached high degree of value to fearlessness. His worthy son, Guru Gobind Singh, literally acted on the principle enunciated by him :

Not to frighten anyone,
Nor to be afraid !

Religious persecution was not the only evil which the Guru fought and countered. He acted with equal measure of vigour and crusading spirit in the region of ignorance and superstition. He reproached those who worshipped stones and placed them on their heads. He criticized those 'who put shiva-lingam around their necks', those who 'saluted effigies', those who bowed before the dead bodies and foolishly indulged in such thoughtless deeds in search of God. He did not permit worship of the graves and tombs, or observance of *jantra, mantra, tantra.* He even remarked—God is not in the sacred books, neither in the *Purān* nor in the *Qurān.* He exhorted men to think straight. "Let passions be subordinated, let Reason dominate," —this forms part of the daily prayer prescribed for the Sikhs. His aspiration seemed to be to compose a community of clear-headed, enlightened individuals. Enlightenment was indeed one of the cherished virtues the Guru desired to promote in human life.

It is a sad commentary on our social dynamics of the past two or three centuries that the good work done by the Gurus was practically lost upon us. Guru Nanak was born in 1469, that is exactly four hundred years earlier than the birth of Mahatma Gandni in 1869. The movement initiated by Nanak and Kabir to discredit the caste-system and bring about a cultural renaissance in India, was continued by the succeeding Gurus; it blossomed in Guru Gobind Singh's time. But the rot soon set in; the caste-system re-emerged with all its ugly manifestations, in the land of the Gurus. Gandhi had to start the struggle all over again to rejuvenate the values suspended in the intervening decades, and to lay the foundations of a society in which all men are brothers. If the intellectual leaders of the international society are inspired by the ideal of brave new world, and if they are really keen to convert their utopian dreams into a living reality, they cannot afford to ignore the rich heritage of the generations past; they cannot help feeling proud of the contributions made to the cultural and spiritual uplift of mankind by the enlightened leaders of all nations; they cannot ignore the principles of dignified human conduct enunciated by savants like Guru Gobind Singh.

10

Guru Gobind Singh's Concept of Nation

In the poetry of the *Dasam Granth*, one finds numerous references to the communities and nationalities of the world. The motivating spirit behind its compilation, Guru Gobind Singh, makes repeated mention of the peoples inhabiting various regions and countries, the languages they speak and the rites and customs they follow. "The Persians, the *ferangis* and the colourful men of France, the instrumentalists of Makrān, the dwellers of Bhakhār, Kandhār and Ghaur, the Gakhars and the Gurdezis" are counted among those who sing praises of the divine Spirit. Mention is made of *Purabis* of the eastern provinces, Hingula of the Himalayan region, Gurdezis and yogis, the Arabs and the French, Kandharis and Kureshis, people of the West, Marathas, Drāvars and Telugus, Bengālis of Bang, *ferangis* of Europe, kings of Dillī, Rohellas of Rohelkhand, Maghelās of Maghda, warriors of Bangash and Bundhelkhand, Gurkhas and Chinese, Manchurians and Tibetans. Listed among languages and dialects are the Arabic, Torki and Persian; Pehlavi, Pushto and Sanskrit; Deshbhakha and Deva-Vāni.

Employing an abundance and affluence of words of the same species, in stanza after stanza, Guru Gobind Singh not only creates a spell-binding effect on his reader, but floods him with information about the multiplicity of the variegated human life and culture. He compliments his Lord thus :

Here Thou art a heavenly singer, a matchless instrumentalist, a Yaksha, the wise, and there a snake, a ghost or a goblin.
Here Thou art a Hindu dwelling, in silence, upon the Gayatri and there a Turk shouting out your call to prayer.

... ...

Now Thou art in arms, now dwelling upon knowledge, now feeding on air, now a companion of beauty.
Now Thou art the speech of angels, the goddess of learning, then the goddess of power and death; now blue-hued, now white.

—(*Akāl Ustati*)

The reader is afforded an insight into the wealth of knowledge and information of detail the Guru possessed. He finds some people reading the Kok-Shāstra, others studying the code of ethics; some are going through the Nyāya-Shāstra, others are learning the rules of battle-field. Some devote themselves to the study of Logic and become experts of Nyāya; some study the Yajurveda, and some others the verses of Brahmā; here some people read the book of Patanjali (*Yogashastra*), there the book of Kanāda (*Vaisheshika Darshan*); and there are others who seek the treasures of knowledge in all the 'fourteen regions'.

Such depiction of the diversity of people's culture illustrates Guru Gobind Singh's image of the communities inhabiting Asian, West Asian and European countries of the late seventeenth-century world. It further illustrates his image of the nationalities inhabiting the Indian sub-continent. The Moghuls had been trying to unify and enlarge the empire, which touched its peak during Aurangzeb's regime. There were still states and territories which, though outside the Moghul empire, formed part of Bhāratvarsha. An Indian State in the modern sense of the term was not in existence in those days. However, some sort of territorial India, with definite Indian traditions, was there. This consciousness of the territory and the spiritual and cultural history of the people had engendered in the native population a sense of nationalism, strong enough to mobilize resistance to the expansionist ambitions of the Moghul rulers.

It is evident from the references contained in Guru Gobind Singh's poetry that the concept of a nation in the 'political' sense had not yet crystallized during his day. In fact, the policies relating to domestic or external affairs of the successive Moghul governments were neither based on national principles nor dictated by national interests. Generally the class and communal interests or the motives of the territorial expansion were involved in the determination of policies. We can hardly speak of the Hindus of northern and southern India and the Muslim settlers in the country, during the Mughal period, as one nation. Even in the West, enthusiasm for the 'national' state took roots after the French Revolution, and gathered momentum during the nineteenth century, when symbols like national flag and national anthem, national language and schooling, national holidays and heroes came to be evolved. The preceding centuries, both in India and the West had known nationalism of an ethnic type. For instance, Jews were a nation though scattered over distant lands. They were bound by common sentiments and beliefs, rather than by a common State. Their members, wherever they were, formed one cultural group; they represented a distinct national character in the lands of their domicile. Even in the present age, Indian or Chinese or Americans abroad represent their respective national patterns of life; although in many cases, people of one national origin settled in another part of the world, gradually come to be absorbed by the State that accepts them.

Factors and elements that combine to create civilization are practically the same as help in producing a basic social group or a national unit. History of national formations and history of civilization are not incongruous. The *ethos* and *mores* of the Indian people that survived the upheavals of ages and furnished historical continuity to Indian civilization, put the stamp of a definite nationality on the Indian people. National spirit, in this context, implied enthusiasm about the people's *ethos;* national literature was literature inspiring love for the traditional values. An appeal to the sentiments and beliefs of the people proved effective, particularly at times of crisis or invasion, or confrontation with a new and rising faith. What was attempted by Kabir and Nanak was a cultural renaissance, a reorientation of the values of ancient India. What Guru Gobind Singh attempted almost two centuries later was again a revival of the spiritual tradition, resurrection of the heroic elements in human character, and rekindling of a passion for protecting the national culture.

Evidently, the nationalism of Guru Gobind Singh's conception was a liberal, humanitarian nationalism, as opposed to the modern nationalism of intense type, leading to alliance of economic and political power, growing strength of the State and pervassive influence over all intellectual and social developments. Nationalism of the olden variety engendered belief in the unity of civilization; it gave rise to feelings of cosmopolitanism. Echoes of these feelings are perceptible in Guru Gobind Singh's verse, wherein mankind is recognized as 'one single race'. The fierce nationalism of today, more often than not, conveniently ignores the common links capable of forging unity between nations. Nations have drifted apart under the impact of nationalism, which some serious thinkers have termed 'a grave evil' and 'a source of appalling danger' in the present set-up of the world.

Another feature of the Indian nationalism of earlier times was its pre-occupation with the internal affairs of the country. Indians were concerned with the way of life that prevailed inside their territory, and with the defence of it. No foreign influence of conquest could completely curb the spirit of nationalism. It appeared time and again, under the leadership of Rana Pratap, and Shivaji, and Guru Gobind Singh. During the days of British expansion, it arose in the form of 1857 war of liberation. Yet, seldom an attempt was made at imposing the Indian way of life on the non-Indian neighbours by force. Nationalist fervour was confined to the upholding of the dignity of an unbroken continuity of culture, even by the use of violence. As Guru Gobind Singh wrote in the *Zafarnāmā* addressed to emperor Aurangzeb :

> When an affair is past every other remedy,
> It is righteous indeed to unsheath the sword.

The nation needed strength of arms not for the sake of subjugating other peoples, but for defending the right of loving its own pattern of life, its art and literature, its linguistic niceties.

its contribution to civilization. The Guru invoked the valiant and fearless aspect of the supreme power, as well as furnished his followers with volumes of heroic literature, in order to inculcate in them the virtues of valour and wisdom.

The Guru seems to have been acutely conscious of the need of leadership a nation has. His whole effort to organize the 'Khālsā,' the select band of disciplined saint-soldiers, with an executive council of 'five chosen ones' at its hand, was clearly directed to this end. The *Khālsā* was designed to give the nation lead in social and political affairs, as also in moral and spiritual regions. An inexhaustible source of inspiration and enlightenment was also placed at the disposal of the nation, in the form of the *Adi Granth* installed as the Guru. Thus the Indian people were fortified by a book as their guide, a workable pattern of organization and leadership, complete with a code of conduct and a set of principles and institutions. The Guru was careful enough to provide a symbol for the nation too—in the form of *Khandā* (the double-edged sword) which not only is a source of courage, but is a symbolic instrument with which to cut asunder darkness and see the light of Truth.

If we look at the phenomenon of nation in the light of Guru Gobind Singh's concept of Time, its true significance as an event in the historical and cosmological perspective becomes all the more clear. According to his philosophy of Time, 'all events are subject to time', i.e. they are the creation of historical process; 'only one Event is Eternal or Timeless,' i.e. not subject to the creative process: This view is repeated several times in the *Dasam Granth*, For instance—

In Time did Brahmā assume a form,
In time did Shiva come down below,
In time did Vishnu reveal himself,
Of Time is all this wondrous show.

(Chaupai, Trans. S.S. Sekhon)

If the wondrous show of the world, with all its events, all its places and all directions are the creation of Time, and if powers like Brahmā and Vishnu, Shiva and Yogis, angels and heavenly beings, all were created in the course of Time and are subject to Time, then nations also come and go, civilizations rise and fall, cultures appear and disappear. The individual who comes to acquire such a perspective, who is imbued with the sense of time and timelessness, can indeed function effectively, be it in the performing of his duty towards the nation, or be it in serving and promoting the cause of humanity, at any particular point of the world-history.

All the characteristics of Nation in the ethnic and cultural sense of the term are available in the compositions attributed to Guru Gobind Singh. He does not portray 'nation' as a Nation-State, nor does he advocate 'internationalism' in the current sense of inter-state relationships, which is of recent origin. Today we talk of nationalism and internationalism not being irreconciable, if internationalism is developed in the sphere to which it belongs (that of economics, politics and war), and if nation of the world stop placing their own interest above that of the world at large. Such a concept had not yet originated when the Guru flourished three centuries ago. But the concept of cosmopolitanism was present; it makes a positive appeal as a forerunner of today's internationalism. The liberal nationalism of pre-State variety, advocated and defended in the Dasam-Granth poetry, accords well with the cosmopolitan outlook and sentiment. It also provides cultural foundation for the establishment of an international humanitarian society, free from inter-state rivalries and conflicts.

11

Moral Philosophy of Baba Farid

Sheikh Farid is regarded as the first recorded poet of the Punjabi language. Spiritual and ethical are the two chief currents in his poetry. In both, his profound love for man and his humanitarianism have taken expression in a style coloured with feelings. Apart from the couplets and hymns composed by Farid in Punjabi, some quotations have been given by Dr. K. A. Nizami in reference to his works extant in Persian, portraying him purely as a moral thinker. Whatever inspiration for spiritual advancement is available in his precepts, its purpose too seems to provide moral strength to man. The teaching contained in the Persian sources has close resemblance with the moral essence of his Punjabi compositions, although the former abounds in gems of worldly wisdom as well, which of course may not be in consonance with the general spiritual-ethical temper of his verse. Here it is proposed to take Farid's compositions in Punjabi as the basis for a study of his ethical philosophy.

The human situation

Mankind, as depicted in the couplets and hymns of Farid, is caught up in a situation of moral crisis that calls for serious thinking and search for a way out. Man finds himself lost in an attractive but meaningless world, which is called by Farid: 'duni suhāvā bāg'— (a pleasing garden). The bird spends the night in the garden like a guest, and just at day-break flies off to a new destination. Should it become evident that after all man is to depart from here, and is not to return, he would not do harm to himself by indulging in this 'false world'. Farid's point of view is supported by Guru Arjan thus: "O Farid, the heart is absorbed in this world, but the world is of no avail." Man's mundane course is full of worry and despair; it is sharper than the edge of a sword. The 'dawn' has broken; it is time to think of marching ahead. But the world, according to Farid, is such a concealed fire that permits no thought, no knowledge.

What is human life?—"A sapling by the river-side: how long shall it endure? O Farid, how long will the unbaked vessel hold the water?" In this life, worry is the bedstead. suffering the bed-strings, and pangs of separation the sheets and quilt. The poor man wastes half of the day in filling the belly and decorating the body, and the other half he wastes in sleep. With the onset of old age, the physique turns weak: one may live up to hundred years—"in the end, the body will turn into dust." Those with pomp and show, the rulers and kings, the in-dwellers of lofty mansions and palaces, all have finally been buried under the earth, on the conclusion of the false bargain of life. Asks Farid —"Where are the parents who gave birth to you?" Knowing all this, you still remain unconvinced? In spite of this awareness, you are carrying, like others, the burden of worldliness. Man seems not to realize the value of time: when the opportunity was to 'earn', he kept engrossed with worldly attachments; when it was time to put on the sails, he failed to make use of the tackle; how will the boat sail safely over the rough waters now? The affairs of life are a source of anguish; better if the midwife, while snipping the umbilical cord, would also press a little the throat. But anguish is not in my lot alone, the entire world is in the grip of suffering.—"Seen from the house-top, each home would appear burning in the same fire." Here, the comment of Guru Arjan reads: "Farid, the earth is full of pleasing colour; in its midst is a garden of poison; those blessed with the Master's grace, will not come to grief."

The body of man is not stable either. Farid has repeatedly called attention to the grey beard and white hair, which remind one of the end that is fast approaching, and the past receding behind. The eyes and ears have turned feeble, the legs unfit to walk; the very appearance of the body has changed; all dallying has ceased. 'Farid, the hair on your head, the beard, as also the moustache—all show signs of decline. O ignorant fool, how dare you still indulge in pleasures?" Nowhere in the world is permanence to be seen; the seasons undergo change, spring giving place to autumn; the physical body too will be reduced to a mere skeleton; the day will come when the crows peck at the limbs of the corpse. Look at the self-delusion of man: he still trots about carefree. When unawares the eagles prey upon him, all joy and idle play will vanish; the angel of death will then take care of this three-and-half-maund body. In youth there is lot of pride and freedom from care, but when the fragrance of youth is gone, a lump of foul-odour *hing* alone will remain. The forgetful mind knows not, the dust will one day eat into the head itself; the poor fellow is worried about his turban getting soiled.

What is the destiny of man, what is his fate ? The devil has so misled him, he listens not to a word of advice or a counsel wise. Scores of self-styled advisers are around; a friend indeed is rare to find. Farid is worried over this misfortune of man; he is anxious to pull him out from this hopeless condition. The ethics of Farid does not consist in his analysis of the human situation and the warning he administers; rather, he offers the gist of his life-long experience, through his couplets and hymns, in the form of moral principles. Farid has no better course to offer in order to liberate man from the mental agony and anguish.

Moral Principles

Self-control is the central theme in Baba Farid's ethical teaching, which takes expression in a variety of forms. To quote a few instances :

> O Farid, make 'even' the surface of your mind,
> Doing away its ups and downs....

O Farid, set not your heart on the towering
mansions and palaces....

O Farid, yearn not after the delicacies consumed by others....

Sheikh Farid could have communion (with God) today.
Only if the cranes of passion, born of his mind, were seized.

A balanced state of the mind, unaffected by pleasure and pain, passion and lust, free from cravings of the body and cranes of desire, is the moral ideal of Baba Farid. Guru Arjan lends support to this end: "O Farid, treat pleasure and pain alike, cleansing the heart of evil and sin." One needs to expend the limited store of life judiciously; let not the moment slip past your hands; if the grains of sesame are in small quantity, should we scatter them about? The sages are heard shouting—Permit not yourself to be robbed.

Another aspect of self-control appears in the form of contentment and forbearance. Farid is convinced that the arrow of contentedness does not miss the aim. But man should be a river-full of contentment and not merely a streamlet. He may himself consume the dry crust of bread and cold water, but must adopt towards others the magnanimity of a *darvesh* who possesses the forbearance and patience of the trees. Farid recommends one to be a critic of oneself—

O Farid, if you are possessed of fine intellect
Blacken not the record of anyone;
Bow your head, and look for the shortcomings within.

Why speak ill of anyone, if we have awareness of our own faults? Why hurt someone's feelings by the use of rude speech? If the true Lord resides in all the souls, then why break the heart-jewel of anyone?

One straight and simple, but serious and stringent principle of Farid's ethics is expressed in these words :

O Farid, do good to the evil-doer
And nurse not anger in the heart.

It is a matter of course for man to think evil and do evil to the evil-doer. But, at the moral level the natural propensities must be brought under an enlightened set of rules. Exercising control over rage and vengeance has been a universal precept for moral conduct, which can well serve as the basis of a higher way of life. Farid has also warned against the unbecoming use of force: if you happen to be a stream, do not go on smashing the banks on either side; you too are answerable to someone. Here, the lesson of modesty and humility is evident. One may oneself turn into the grass that is trampled, but let one not humiliate the weak, the lowly, even the dust under one's feet; 'who can stand comparison with dust'? If someone makes an assault on you, you are not to attack him in retaliation. This level of morality demands, perhaps, an unusual courage.

Farid has assigned to the concepts of 'karma' and 'dharma' of the Indian philosophical tradition a place in his ethical system. "Let us ever perform our *dharma* by sticking to the truth and shunning falsehood. Let the disciple follow the path shown by the *guru*." And as regards the fruit of *karma*:..."Those indulging in evil deeds, will receive severe punishment." Similarly, "Avoid the acts, O man, that have no merit in them." The man of virtuous deeds, whose soul is unblemished, remains non-attached while living in the world; he is like the swan who has accidentally come down in the field of chaff, but does not peck at inferior grain. While criticising hypocrisy and pretence, Farid has portrayed the picture of a person who wears the apparel of *faqirs*, speaks softly and sweetly, but inside his mind thinks of wielding the knife.—"Outwardly he seems bright, but within is he the darkness of night." Just as Guru Nanak gives the picture of "Pilgrims going to bathe at holy places, with treacherous bodies and corrupted souls."

Among the moral values, Farid assigns a place of honour to life of freedom, temper of a *faqir*, and love for humanity. The ideal of liberty that democracy has upheld in modern times, already finds a reference in the following couplet of Farid:

O Farid, may I never lose my liberty
Be this the Lord's will;

If I deserve not my independence
Let him put my life to end.

Death is preferable to a life of dependence. But independence does not mean a life of material affluence and indulgence; Farid attaches more value to modest living and a measure of abnegation. When one has little to spare, one may still have the inclination to share with others, and the spirit of sacrifice be present,—only such a one deserves the epithet of *bhakta*. This love for humanity, in Farid's thought, is another form of the love of God. The *bhakta* or *darvesh* has affection for his Master; he is tied in an unbreakable knot of love; he does not permit greed and avarice in his mind, for greed and love cannot go together,—"Greed is the negation of love."

Farid Philosophy

The philosophy of Baba Farid is a synthesis of humanism and theism. His ethical and spiritual currents converge on love for humanity and the Divine. His God is so 'sweet' that none of the sweet objects—shakar, sugar, candy, jaggery, honey, milk—can stand comparison with him. All the pleasant comforts of life may be sacrificed for the sake of such sweet Lord—

I fear not the loss of youth
If love of God be retained.
O Farid, countless youthful looks
For want of love have withered away.

Never mind if one has to pass through muddy streets and rains, or the only woollen rag in possession of the poor man gets wet or soiled on the way. For, whoever belongs to God, the whole world belongs to him. Who else is there to pay heed to our tale of woe? He alone is my protector, otherwise I too would have been burnt to ash by the concealed fire of the world. I have searched through the entire existence, none is found as great as He.

Farid's God is sweet, loving, compassionate, provident, master, magnanimous, and beloved. In the characterization of these personal qualities, Farid-Bāni and Nanak-Bāni correspond to each other. But the concept of the Absolute and Transcendent (*Brahman* and *Agochar*) of the Guru-Bāni does not form part of Farid's philosophy. The spiritualistic approach of Farid is that of a devotee and *bhakta*; it is not the rationalistic spirit of a metaphysician or scholar. Nor does he impart instruction in *sanyāsa* and abandonment. What would you gain by roaming from forest to forest, except for the trampling of thorns ? God resides in the heart itself—"What do you seek in the wilderness ?"

In line with the general tradition of the path of *bhakti*, Sheikh Farid lays stress on worship and prayer. Man is to depart from the world, if not today, tomorrow: "In each one's respective turn, the saint and the sage all must go." Let us better our lot through prayer and worship; the head that bows not before the Lord, "deserves to be chopped off." The lovers separated suffer the pangs of separation, but "sorrow is the king of life,"--the urge for union fails to gain intensity without the pain of separation. Farid is ready to assume whatever course makes it possible to unite him with God: "Let me wear such apparel as brings my Lord in embrace." Here Guru Amardās offered the comment that meeting with the Lord was possible while staying at home putting on the usual dress, "only if one wills in good faith." What words to utter, which qualities to wear, what gem of a formula to adopt, in order to win over the beloved Lord? The speech of humility and modesty, the virtue of forgiveness, and the magic of sweet words—that is the gist of Farid's moral excellence, forming the basis of spiritual attainment.

Baba Farid seems to be keenly aware of the inequitable material distribution in the world. On one hand are people enjoying sumptuous dishes, while others have in their lot the dried crumbs; some have flour to spare, others are without even the salt. But how is a *darvesh* affected by such state of affairs? Even so, Farid makes the ironical remark that—"those who eat delicacies, shall suffer the pains equally intense." The *darvesh* has no concern with such suffering; he is the one traversing the thorny path of the mendicant. Meritorious is the life of a loving devotee, who goes on sharing with others even when he possesses little; who forbears as if he were weak and humble in spite of his might. On the 'name' of God he banks; those who are indifferent to contemplation, are a needless burden on the earth. Farid has not furnished philosophic elaboration of the contemplation of 'name', but this much he points out that the ones soaked in God's love, the devotees completely absorbed in his captivating vision, are followers of Divine contemplation. Those alone are in tune with the truth, who have love lodged in them—

> Truthful are they who love
> From the bottom of their heart.

Index